For every educator who's ever felt weary or unseen, Jochum's words reignite purpose and offer actionable ways to lead and make an impact right from where you are. Educators don't need to become more, who they are is already enough.

Jacki Mjoen
Middle School Math Teacher

Chris is a leading voice in education, and his book doesn't disappoint. Chris lays out a blueprint for stronger leadership in our schools, not by hiring an outside organization but by empowering teachers to realize their potential and their influence on campus. Chris takes the plan from an idea to implementation through a workshop framework, sound advice and practicality. His book is easy to read, and you will find yourself shaking your head in agreement while reading!

Todd Bloomer
Author, Coach, Mentor, Leader, Father, Husband

What an inspiring and rich collection of wisdom for the game-changing focus on Teacher Leaders and the reality and potential to impact and change lives by the thousands. With a rich, well researched, and practical framework provided by an exemplar practitioner, Chris provides credible, practical, and impactful insights into a role that can easily drive transformative impact.

As we know from decades of research in the world of education, those districts that stand out know the role of Teacher Leaders is a critical difference maker at the building and district level–and on generational impact. Thanks for also highlighting that the belief and mindset of teachers as leaders is real–and it starts at the top with leading by example.

Brad Black
President and CEO

Dr. Jochum reminds us that true leadership begins in the classroom. *You Don't Have to Leave to Lead* honors the influence teachers already possess and offers a clear, practical path to strengthen that impact. Every educator will find both encouragement and empowerment in these pages. This book is a thoughtful, actionable guide for anyone who wants to lead right where they are.

Martin Silverman
Author, Coach, Consultant, Educator

I highly recommend Dr. Jochum's book to both current and aspiring leaders. Each section demonstrates Dr. Jochum's deep expertise.

Dr. Matt Seimears
President, Lower Columbia College

The importance of teacher leadership has long been recognized, but support for teacher leaders remains underdeveloped. This volume fills the urgent need for a research-based, practice-focused resource for teacher leaders and for administrators who support them. Decades of research are very ably summarized as a foundation, and years of experience in leader development inform chapters that provide practical guidance while at the same time inviting productive reflection. This book should be read by prospective teachers, in-service teachers, as well as by the faculty who prepare them and the administrators who support them. It provides the vision and the practical supports needed to strengthen individual teachers and the teaching profession.

Mark LaCelle-Peterson
President, Association for Advancing Quality in Educator Preparation

You Don't have to Leave to Lead is a refreshing reminder that leadership isn't about titles, it's about purpose. Dr. Jochum captures the heart of teacher leadership, which is grounded in relationships, driven by influence, and sustained by belief in what's possible. He offers a clear, practical framework that helps educators see themselves as the leaders they already are and gives them the tools to turn that belief into action.

Megan Diede
Speaker, Author, Consultant

Dr. Jochum's *You Don't Have to Leave to Lead* redefines what it means to lead as an educator. Grounded in research and rich with real-world insight, it celebrates the power teachers already hold to shape culture and inspire change without stepping away from their students. Dr. Jochum embodies the character, courage, and heart he writes about, making this book both a reflection of his leadership and an invitation for others to lead where they are.

Tabatha Rosproy
2020 Kansas and National Teacher of the Year

Over the past 10 years, I have advocated for teacher leadership and voice in school districts. You Don't Have to Leave to Lead gives a roadmap on how to do this and captures the essence of what great teaching and leadership are all about —service, influence, and purpose. Dr. Jochum reminds us that true leadership begins in the classroom, where teachers inspire change and build capacity every day. His work provides both practical tools and renewed vision for empowering educators to lead from their current position. This book is a powerful affirmation that the heart of leadership in education beats strongest in our teachers.

Randy Watson, EdD
Kansas Commissioner of Education

Chris Jochums delivers a masterclass in leadership with *You Don't Have to Leave to Lead*. This book is a game changer for teachers who want to influence culture without leaving the classroom. His workshop-style chapters make leadership development feel both accessible and actionable. Chris reminds educators that impact doesn't require a title–just courage, reflection, and purpose. This is the roadmap for every teacher ready to lead where they are.

Dan Stecken
Superintendent, Author, Creator of ~~stressed~~ Leaders Retreat

Chris Jochum's *You Don't Have to Leave to Lead* is an empowering and practical guide that reminds educators their influence begins in the classroom. Drawing on research and experiences Jochum provides actionable strategies to help teachers lead with purpose and impact from within their schools. The book celebrates educators as already enough–equipped with the mindset and ability to drive meaningful change. Inspiring and deeply grounded in practice, it's a must-read for anyone seeking to strengthen leadership and community in education.

Jim Sutfin
Retired Superintendent

Chris Jochum gets it. He understands that leadership in education isn't about titles, it's about influence, courage, and service. *You Don't Have to Leave to Lead* shines a powerful light on the leadership already living inside our classrooms. As someone who has spent my career helping schools strengthen culture, climate, and commitment, I can tell you this book is a must-read for every educator who wants to make a difference right where they stand. It's real, it's practical, and it will remind you why you chose this work in the first place.

Stand Tall Steve Bollar
Education Leadership Expert, Author, Speaker

A powerful, research-based guide that empowers teachers to lead from where they are. Dr. Jochum blends timeless scholarship with actionable strategies and reflection, inspiring educators to grow with confidence, clarity, and purpose. A must-read for every teacher ready to elevate their influence and impact within their classroom and with colleagues and school community.

David Arencibia, EdD
Author, Speaker, Trainer, National Principal of the Year Finalist

In an era when teachers are being asked to do more than ever before, *You Don't Have to Leave to Lead: A Practical Guide to Teacher Leadership* arrives as both a breath of fresh air and a powerful call to action. It reminds us that leadership in education does not require stepping away from the classroom—it begins right where we already stand.

What makes this book exceptional is its unwavering belief in the capacity of teachers to lead from within. The author provides a clear, practical, and inspiring roadmap for educators who want to expand their influence while remaining deeply connected to students and instruction.

Most importantly, this book redefines teacher leadership not as "one more thing" to do, but as a transformative mindset—one that empowers educators to lead with purpose, elevate their colleagues, and positively shape the culture and climate of their schools.

Rodrick S. Lucero, PhD
Executive Director/Professor, Texas A&M University
President/CEO, National Center for Clinical Practice in Educator Preparation

YOU DON'T HAVE TO LEAVE TO LEAD

A Practical Guide to Teacher Leadership

DR. CHRISTOPHER J. JOCHUM

You Don't Have to Leave to Lead: A Practical Guide to Teacher Leadership

Copyright © by Dr. Christopher J. Jochum
First Edition 2025

All rights reserved.

No part of this publication may be reproduced in any form, or by any means, electronic or mechanical, including photocopying, recording, or any information browsing, storage or retrieval system, without permission in writing from the publisher.

Road to Awesome, LLC.

TABLE OF CONTENTS

Preface — 1

Chapter 1 — 7
Why Teacher Leadership Matters

Chapter 2 — 25
Developing and Supporting Teacher Leaders

Chapter 3 — 39
Roles and Goals of Teacher Leadership

Chapter 4 — 55
Teacher Leader Standards: A Model of Success

Chapter 5 — 69
The Teacher-Leader's Credo

Chapter 6 — 89
Developing your Mission Statement

Chapter 7 — 111
Leadership is a Day Job

Chapter 8 — 135
The Power of Relationships

Chapter 9 — 155
Culture and Climate: We All Live Here

Chapter 10 — 179
Identifying Core Values

Chapter 11 — 199
Addressing Conflict with Courage, Comfort and Consistency

Chapter 12 — 227
Relational Realities of Leadership

Conclusion — 243

PREFACE

A few years ago, I attended an education conference that gathered PreK-12 educators and those like me who train future teachers at the university level. During one of the social networking breaks, I overheard someone approach an individual I assumed was a friend or former colleague and say, "Hey! I haven't seen you since you left to take that administrative job. How are things going?" The other person replied, "OK. I actually wish I could still be in the classroom more, but, you know, I always wanted to get into leadership, so I didn't have a choice."

As someone who works in both the teacher education field and also studies leadership, I thought about that brief interaction for the rest of the conference, sharing it with my friends and colleagues, trying to determine if most PreK-12 teachers truly believed that the only way to be a leader was to leave the classroom and assume a formalized title as an administrator.

As a fortunate coincidence, I was not only in the early stages of writing a leadership book for university-level department chairs, but I had also been asked to develop and teach a special topics class as part of our teacher education honors program. Consequently, I decided to offer the class on teacher leadership.

Now, over five years and a few hundred students later, I have taught teacher leadership to pre-and in-service teachers, provided on-site professional development, and served as a keynote speaker on the topic. As a result, I am convinced that developing and supporting teacher leaders is an untapped, often unrealized resource in many of our schools.

Through this experience, I have also confirmed what I overheard at that conference: many teachers believe they must leave the classroom and change their professional title to be considered a leader. This reveals a lack of understanding and appreciation for the inherent leadership acumen and potential teachers already possess; they don't have to leave to lead.

Research shows that developing and empowering teacher leaders *supports increased student achievement, helps recruit and retain qualified teachers, increases teachers' job satisfaction, and helps administrators build capacity within their teams* (see Chapter 1). However, I'm not implying that, by itself, this is the magic bullet for all of the current challenges and concerns in PreK-12 education.

Furthermore, as I write this, I am in my ninth year as the chair of a large teacher education department, which serves over 900 students. Since we are fortunate to have a robust online program that enables us to place students almost anywhere in the United States and abroad, I routinely work with administrators and teachers in schools and districts of all sizes and profiles. Accordingly, I appreciate and understand the many challenges our PreK-12 colleagues face, not the least of which is a significant teacher shortage coupled with more teachers leaving the profession. I realize that many districts must take a triage approach to hire teachers, and developing teacher leaders may sound as far-fetched as starting the school year fully staffed with experienced, licensed teachers!

Nonetheless, I'm reminded of the well-known story "Acres of Diamonds," which tells the tale of an African farmer who, after hearing of the riches other farmers had made by leaving home and discovering diamond mines, sold his farm and set out to find his fortune. Meanwhile, the man who bought his farm soon discovered that it was, in fact, one of the largest diamond mines in all of Africa. The first farmer who ultimately never found his fortune failed to realize that the entire time he was dreaming of what riches he might find elsewhere he was literally standing on acres of diamonds; he just never took the time to uncover them.

I believe each and every school has its own uncovered acres of diamonds with professional educators who want to stay in the classroom while also being given opportunities to lead and grow.

Purpose and Format of the Book

I wrote this book for teachers, those currently in the classroom and future educators preparing to enter the profession. Whether you're already in the classroom or preparing to become a teacher, you are (or soon will be) a leader who makes decisions that impact young lives daily. This book will help you grow professionally and expand your influence throughout your school, district and community. Leadership isn't about titles—it's about character, courage, relationships, and service—qualities you demonstrate every day as an educator. Although primarily written for teachers, this book is also for administrators interested in developing and supporting teacher leaders within their respective schools and districts.

This book is organized in two parts. The first four chapters lay the foundation with research-backed definitions, standards, and frameworks for teacher leadership. While I've kept the tone conversational and practical, this research base is essential for understanding how developing and supporting teacher leaders can transform schools and empower educators.

Chapters 5 through 12 focus on development and are structured like a workshop series. Here you'll find actionable strategies you can implement immediately in your classroom and school. While still grounded in research, these chapters emphasize practical steps to grow your leadership capacity and expand your influence.

Each chapter builds on the previous one, offering functional strategies, reflective exercises, and actionable steps, whether you're reading independently or as part of a group. The principles and frameworks will help you develop the leadership potential you already possess, thus enhancing your professional impact.

I also hope this book reaffirms and renews your sense of purpose, passion, and energy as a professional educator. While some readers may use it to explore paths to formal leadership positions like administration, others will find value in strengthening their leadership within their current role. Wherever your professional journey leads, I'm confident this book will help you appreciate and develop your leadership ability and potential.

How to Use This Book

Whether you're a teacher or administrator reading this on your own, or as part of a larger group or team, the following are effective ways to use this book:

Personal Development

Use this book as your personal guide to discovering and developing your leadership potential while remaining in the classroom or as you seek additional teacher leadership roles.

Professional Learning Communities

Use this as part of a book study in which you collaborate with colleagues to discuss and implement the developmental lessons to enhance your instructional practice and personal leadership journey.

District-Wide Training and Professional Development
Implement this book as part of a comprehensive approach to developing teacher leaders across your school or district, based on the practical frameworks and guiding questions provided in each chapter.

Developing Future Administrators
Either in conjunction with building or district-wide professional development or as a standalone, grow-your-own initiative, school leaders – such as principals and superintendents – can use this book to harvest their own acre of diamonds, building leadership capacity within their own schools and districts, thus contributing to the administrative pipeline.

Higher Education
This book can serve as a primary or supplemental textbook in university courses at the undergraduate level for pre-service teachers, at the graduate level for in-service teachers, and for building and district-level administrators.

Teacher leadership isn't just another initiative or "one more thing" on teachers' plates. Rather, it's a transformative approach that empowers educators while positively contributing to student achievement and schools' organizational culture and climate.

I wrote this book as your colleague. My goal is to add value to you and those you serve by helping you uncover and develop the leadership talent you already possess, thus supporting your desire to make a difference in students' lives from within your classroom. Remember, you don't have to leave to lead!

CHAPTER 1
Why Teacher Leadership Matters

"A leader is one who knows the way,
goes the way, and shows the way."
~John C. Maxwell

Whether you are a current or aspiring teacher or administrator, let me start by asking you three important questions:

1. How do you define leadership?
2. What are some traits and characteristics of effective leaders?
3. Who are the leaders in PreK-12 schools?

In my experience working with future and current teachers, some of whom have been in the classroom for many years, when asked these questions, they typically define leadership as being in charge of other people or being the boss. Additionally, they indicate that effective leaders should be honest, trustworthy, and open-minded. Finally, when asked to identify the leaders in their respective schools and districts, they usually list administrative or titled leadership roles such as assistant principals, principals, and superintendents.

While the aforementioned responses are correct to varying degrees, they are nonetheless incomplete and, in my opinion, represent a common misconception: most teachers do not see themselves as leaders in their respective schools. When asked why, the most common response I hear is, "I'm not a leader. I'm just a teacher." I find this disheartening,

Granted, it takes a village to teach our children; schools must have administrators who hold titled leadership positions and are responsible for directly overseeing and affecting the school culture, climate, and success of those within it (students and staffulty). Furthermore, we continue to need excellent educators with prerequisite classroom experience who feel called to serve in administrative roles, thus supporting the principal pipeline.

At the same time, there seems to be a sense among some teachers, especially those who have already been in the classroom for several years and are interested in additional career opportunities, that the only way to serve as a leader within their respective schools is to transition into administration. They seem to believe they are not leaders until they have an official title and, therefore, must leave the classroom to lead.

Teachers Are Leaders

Contrary to the common misconception that teachers are not schoolwide leaders, extensive research over the past 40 years consistently highlights the significant benefits of developing teacher leaders, which include:

Positive Impact on Student Learning, Success, and School Improvement

Teacher leaders play a crucial role in enhancing educational outcomes and driving schoolwide progress (Bixler & Ceballos, 2023; Handford & Leithwood, 2013; Leithwood & Riehl, 2003; Muijs & Harris, 2006; York-Barr & Duke, 2004).

Recruitment and Retention of Qualified Teachers

Schools with strong teacher leadership are better equipped to attract and retain talented educators, especially in traditionally hard-to-staff or underperforming schools (Behrstock & Clifford, 2009; Coggins & McGovern, 2014; Donaldson, 2007; Johnson & Donaldson, 2004; Morettini, et al., 2 018; National Center for Great Public Schools; Podlosky, et al., 2016).

Increased Job Satisfaction, Confidence, and Professional Purpose for Teachers

Empowered teacher leaders experience greater fulfillment and commitment to their profession (Beachum & Dentith, 2004; Chesson, 2011; Friedman, 2011; Hunzicker, 2012; Vernon-Dotson & Floyd, 2011).

Improved Collaboration, Self-Efficacy, and Pedagogical Content Knowledge Among Teachers

Teacher leaders foster a collaborative environment that enhances teaching practices and teacher confidence (Curtis, 2013; Hofstein, et al., 2004; Muijs & Harris, 2003, 2006; Sing, et al., 2012; Wenner & Campbell, 2017; York-Barr & Duke, 2004).

Development of a Culture and Climate of Professionalism and Empowerment Among Teachers

Teacher leadership cultivates a professional community where teachers feel valued and empowered (Beachum & Dentith, 2004; Chesson, 2011; Edge & Mylopoulos, 2008; Hofstein, et al., 2004; Vernon-Dotson, 2011).

Support for Administration by Building Capacity Among Faculty and Aspiring Administrators

Teacher leaders not only support current school leaders but also help in nurturing the next generation of educational administrators (Brooks, et al., 2004; Crowther, et al., 2009; Leithwood & Mascall, 2008).

Although the challenges faced by schools can vary and be rather nuanced, review the benefits of developing teacher leaders. *How many teachers, administrators, staff, and related stakeholders in a given school or district would want to positively impact student success while retaining quality teachers who find increased job satisfaction housed in an organizational climate of professionalism, empowerment, and collaboration?* By recognizing and promoting teacher leadership, schools can leverage these benefits to create a more effective and supportive educational environment.

While it is neither my contention nor the premise of this book that developing teacher leaders is a panacea for the challenges within our schools, I firmly believe it is an important variable that has perhaps been overlooked.

In their book *Awakening the Sleeping Giant: Helping Teachers Develop as Leaders*, Marilyn Katzenmeyer and Gayle Moller (2009) support this notion with the following:

"Within every school there is a sleeping giant of teacher leadership, which can be a strong catalyst for making change. By using the energy of teacher leaders as agents of school change, the reform of public education will stand a better chance of building momentum." (p. 69)

Additionally, there are standards associated with teacher preparation, professional development, and instructional evaluation. These standards specifically focus on and/or require the development of teacher leaders due to the impact on students, teachers, and the school climate. A few notable standards can be found in Charlotte Danielson's *Framework for Teaching Evaluation Instrument* (2013), the *Council of Chief State School Officers InTASC Standards* (2013), and the *Teacher Leader Model Standards* (2011).

While the support for developing teacher leaders and the associated benefits are well-documented within the educational literature, it's also important to understand the various definitions of teacher leadership that have emerged.

Defining Teacher Leadership

In their seminal article, "What Do We Know About Teacher Leadership? Findings From Two Decades of Scholarship," researchers York-Barr and Duke (2004) define teacher leadership as "the process by which teachers, individually or collectively influence their colleagues, principals, and other members of school communities to improve teaching and learning practices with the aim of increased student learning and achievement" (pp. 287-288).

Influenced by York-Barr and Duke's work, subsequent research over the past 20 years has offered additional definitions of teacher leadership:

- "Those persons, occupying various roles in the school, who provide direction and exert influence in order to achieve the school's goals" (Leithwood & Riehl, 2003, p. 2).
- "Teacher leaders model effective practices, exercise their influence in formal and informal contexts, and support collaborative team structures within their schools" (Teacher Leadership Exploratory Consortium, 2011, p. 11).
- "A teacher whose official schedule includes both teaching K–12 students and leading teachers in some capacity" (Margolis, 2012, p. 292).
- "Teacher leaders lead within and beyond the classroom; identify with and contribute to a community of teacher learners and leaders; influence others toward improved educational practice; and accept responsibility for achieving the outcomes of their leadership" (Katzenmeyer & Moller, 2016, p. 124).
- "Teachers who maintain K-12 classroom-based teaching responsibilities, while also taking on leadership responsibilities outside of the classroom" (Wenner & Campbell, 2017, p. 140).
- "Individuals who use their gifts and talents to create a positive impact on student learning and school/community culture inside and outside the classroom" (Matsumoto, et al., 2018, p. 202).

Defining Leadership

As Dee Hock, founder and CEO of the Visa credit association, once said, "...leadership is leadership" (*Leadership Quotes*, n.d.). While this provides an undeniably accurate and simple definition, I believe it is important to provide additional definitions to better frame teacher leaders' development and application throughout this book.

I define leadership as influence through character, courage, relationships, and service, which I have developed through my experiences, academic preparation, and research (Jochum, 2021, p. 59). Additionally, I firmly believe that *leadership is the one thing that can change everything* within almost every organization.

The data overwhelmingly support this notion. For example, worldwide research by Gallup shows that managers (leaders) account for 70% of the variance in employee engagement (Back & Harter, 2023). This influence is profound; it can be an organization's greatest asset or its most critical liability. On one hand, poor leadership drives talent away due to its negative influence. In fact, some studies identify managers as the primary reason that three out of every four employees voluntarily leave their jobs (Robinson, 2022).

Conversely, this highlights the immense positive power of effective leadership. If poor leadership repels talent, great leadership attracts and retains it. By building organizational engagement and trust, great leaders become an organization's most critical factor for stability and success. This is precisely why, as John Maxwell, one of the world's foremost leadership experts, often says, "Everything rises and falls on leadership" (Maxwell, 2011, p. 106).

One definition that is particularly powerful to all leaders and especially applicable to teachers is Brené Brown's. Brown, a world-renowned author, researcher, speaker, and professor who studies courageous leadership, shame, and vulnerability, defines a leader as "anyone who takes responsibility for finding the potential in people and processes and who has the courage to develop that potential" (Brown, 2018, p. 4).

Let's unpack Dr. Brown's definition within the context of serving as a classroom teacher by addressing these questions:

1. As a teacher, how often do you take responsibility for finding the potential in your students, both as individuals and academically?
2. As a teacher, how often does "taking responsibility and finding potential" in your students involve processes, procedures, and habits?
3. As a teacher, how often do you have to show courage (i.e., be uncomfortable in the service of others) as part of developing your students' potential?

Finding Potential in Others

Is it part of your job to find potential in your students? Of course, it is! My experience as a classroom teacher and education professor suggests that finding and developing potential in our students is something we must do daily, which can be as rewarding as it is challenging. How many times have you and your colleagues felt a sense of pride because a student overcame some obstacle to achieve something remarkable?

Likewise, how often have you been worried or even disappointed at the thought of a student not reaching their full potential? Like most teachers, you've probably put in extra hours, spent your own money, and lost sleep trying to ensure that all your kids could succeed. Finding and developing potential in others is what teachers do!

Processes, Procedures, and Habits

When you were studying to be a teacher in college, I'm fairly confident you were asked to develop robust lesson plans and supporting assessments. These plans probably followed a template that required you to show alignment with state standards, account for the needs of diverse learners, and perhaps have an extra activity planned just in case you needed more time.

I would also guess that like most developing or preservice teachers, yours truly included, the first time you taught your 20-page lesson plan, which was designed to last 50 minutes, you were thrilled that you covered it all but didn't know what to do with the remaining 40 minutes of the class period!

Now that you are an experienced teacher, you can write a few keywords on a notepad to remind yourself of what you will teach. Furthermore, despite not taking the time to write a multi-page lesson plan using a prescribed template, I do not doubt that your lessons, classroom instruction, and assessments are exemplary. Almost without thinking, you know how to start your class effectively, make seamless transitions, and, most importantly, make on-the-spot decisions to account for the unexpected. I also suspect that in the first few years of teaching, you developed eyes in the back of your head and intuitively know what's going on (or what's about to happen) in your classroom at all times.

As a teacher, you have developed a series of processes, procedures, and habits, many of which are now second nature, that directly and positively affect your ability to be responsible for and uncover the potential in your students. Although I don't know exactly how you responded to question two, I imagine you were somewhat surprised at just how many structures you have in place that are now intuitive, minute-by-minute habits directly supporting your students' achievement.

Being Uncomfortable for Others

How did you answer question three, which asked how often you must be courageous as a teacher? Were you surprised at the frequency with which you're willing to step up and be uncomfortable in support of your students' development and potential?

While there are many ways to define courage, in simple terms, I define it as the extent to which people are willing to be uncomfortable to positively serve and affect others. Accordingly, I believe all classroom teachers are courageous, whether they realize it or not.

It takes courage to effectively manage a classroom by addressing students' choices and conduct, which oftentimes requires having difficult conversations. It takes courage to make a phone call or send an email to a parent, which may upset them and open the door to additional conflict. It takes courage to advocate for your students, especially if it requires engaging in an uncomfortable conversation with colleagues and/or administrators. Ultimately, it takes courage to get up and dedicate your life to teaching and serving kids each and every day.

In reviewing Brené Brown's definition of leadership, one would be hard-pressed to make a case that teachers are not the epitome of leadership. Moreover, while every adult who works in a school, to some degree, has influence over and contributes to students' education and well-being, teachers, on a day-by-day, minute-by-minute basis, take responsibility for courageously and consistently engaging in processes designed to find and develop students' potential. Not only are teachers leaders, but they are also arguably the most influential leaders in our schools.

Whether you are reading this as a future or current classroom teacher or administrator, I hope you now understand the value and hidden treasure – the sleeping giants – that training and supporting teacher leaders can provide students and all stakeholders associated with their educational journey. Remember, it's not about the title; it's about influence! You don't have to leave the classroom to lead.

Discussion and Application Questions

1. Before reading this chapter, to what extent did you know the value of developing teacher leaders, as supported by the research?
2. In the first three questions asked in this chapter, how did you respond to "Who are the leaders in PreK-12 schools?" Did you include yourself or other teachers? Why or why not?
3. What are three previous assumptions this chapter either reinforced or caused you to reconsider regarding the value of teacher leadership?
4. What are two questions or concerns you still have?

References

Back, R., & Harter, J. (2023, March 28). Managers account for 70% of variance in employee engagement. *Gallup.* https://news.gallup.com/businessjournal/182792/managers-account-variance-employee-engagement.aspx

Beachum, F., & Dentith, A. M. (2004). Teacher leaders creating cultures of school renewal and transformation. *The Educational Forum, 68*(3), 276–286.

Behrstock, E., & Clifford, M. (2009). *Leading Gen Y teachers: Emerging strategies for school leaders.* National Comprehensive Center for Teacher Quality. https://gtlcenter.org/sites/default/files/docs/February2009Brief.pdf

Bixler, K., & Ceballos, M. (2023). Promoting teacher leadership: Principal actions to promote and facilitate teacher leadership for enhanced student outcomes. *Leading & Managing, 29*(1), 21–30.

Brooks, J. S., Scribner, J. P., & Eferakorho, J. (2004). Teacher leadership in the context of whole school reform. *Journal of School Leadership, 14*(3), 242–265.

Brown, B. (2018). *Dare to lead: Brave work. Tough conversations. Whole hearts.* [Kindle version]. Random House. https://a.co/d/5C2eoSj

Chesson, L. S. (2011). *The nature of teacher leadership in a Boston pilot school* [Doctoral dissertation]. ProQuest Dissertations Publishing.

Coggins, C., & McGovern, K. (2014). Five goals for teacher leadership. *Phi Delta Kappan, 95*(7), 15–21.

Council of Chief State School Officers. (2013). *Interstate Teacher Assessment and Support Consortium InTASC model core teaching standards and learning progressions for teachers 1.0: A resource for ongoing teacher development.*

Crowther, F., Ferguson, M., & Hann, L. (2009). *Developing teacher leaders.* Corwin Press.

Curtis, R. (2013). *Finding a new way: Leveraging teacher leadership to meet unprecedented demands*. Aspen Institute.

Danielson, C. (2013). *The framework for teaching evaluation instrument, 2013 edition*. The Danielson Group.

Donaldson, M. L. (2007). To lead or not to lead? A quandary for newly tenured teachers. In R. H. Ackerman & S. V. Mackenzie (Eds.), *Uncovering teacher leadership: Essays and voices from the field* (pp. 259–272). Corwin Press.

Edge, K., & Mylopoulos, M. (2008). Creating cross-school connections: LC networking in support of leadership and instructional development. *School Leadership & Management, 28*(2), 147–158.

Friedman, H. (2011). The myth behind the subject leader as a school key player. *Teachers and Teaching, 17*(3), 289–302.

Handford, V., & Leithwood, K. (2013). Why teachers trust school leaders. *Journal of Educational Administration, 51*(2), 194–212.

Hofstein, A., Carmeli, M., & Shore, R. (2004). The professional development of high school chemistry coordinators. *Journal of Science Teacher Education, 15*(1), 3–24.

Hunzicker, J. (2012). Professional development and job-embedded collaboration: How teachers learn to exercise leadership. *Professional Development in Education, 38*(2), 267–289.

Jochum, C. J. (2021). *The department chair: A practical guide to effective leadership*. [Kindle version]. Rowman & Littlefield. https://a.co/d/drtNy7W

Johnson, S. M., & Donaldson, M. L. (2004). Sustaining new teachers through professional growth. In S. M. Johnson (Ed.),

Finders and keepers: Helping new teachers survive and thrive in our schools (pp. 225–248). Jossey-Bass.

Katzenmeyer, M., & Moller, G. (2009). *Awakening the sleeping giant: Helping teachers develop as leaders* (3rd ed.). Corwin Press.

Katzenmeyer, M., & Moller, G. (2016). Chapter 13: Understanding teacher leadership. In *Counterpoints* (Vol. 466, pp. 121–136).

Leadership Quotes | LeadingThoughts. (n.d.). *LeadershipNow.com*. https://leadershipnow.com/leadershipquotes3.html

Leithwood, K. A., & Mascall, B. (2008). Collective leadership effects on student achievement. *Educational Administration Quarterly, 44*(4), 529–561.

Leithwood, K. A., & Riehl, C. (2003). *What we know about successful school leadership*. National College for School Leadership.

Margolis, J. (2012). Hybrid teacher leaders and the new professional development ecology. *Professional Development in Education, 38*(2), 291–315.

Matsumoto, V., Yoshioka, J., & Fulton, L. (2018). Cultivating teacher candidates' passions into leadership for tomorrow: The gift that keeps on giving. In J. Hunzicker (Ed.), *Teacher leadership in professional development schools* (pp. 201–216). Emerald Publishing Limited.

Maxwell, J. C. (2011). *The 360 degree leader: Developing your influence from anywhere in the organization*. [Kindle version]. HarperCollins Leadership. https://a.co/d/h9PZnVs

Morettini, B., Luet, K. M., Vernon-Dotson, L., Nagic, N., & Krishnamurthy, S. (2018). Developing teacher leaders using a distributed leadership model: Five signature features of a school–university partnership. In J. Hunzicker (Ed.), *Teacher leadership in professional development schools* (pp. 217–233). Emerald Publishing Limited.

Muijs, D., & Harris, A. (2003). Teacher leadership—Improvement through empowerment? *Educational Management & Administration, 31*(4), 437–448.

Muijs, D., & Harris, A. (2006). Teacher led school improvement: Teacher leadership in the UK. *Teaching and Teacher Education, 22*(8), 961–972.

National Center for Great Public Schools. (n.d.). Teacher leaders. https://cgps.nea.org/greatteaching/career-phases/teacher-leaders/

Podolsky, A., Kini, T., Bishop, J., & Darling-Hammond, L. (2016). *Solving the teacher shortage: How to attract and retain excellent educators.* Learning Policy Institute.

Robinson, J. (2022, December 12). Turning around employee turnover. *Gallup.* https://news.gallup.com/businessjournal/106912/turning-around-your-turnover-problem.aspx

Singh, A., Yager, S., Yutakom, N., Yager, R., & Ali, M. M. (2012). Constructivist teaching practices used by five teacher leaders for the Iowa Chautauqua professional development program. *International Journal of Environmental & Science Education, 7,* 197–216.

Teacher Leadership Exploratory Consortium. (2011). *Teacher leader model standards.* https://www.ets.org/content/dam/ets-org/pdfs/patl/patl-teacher-leader-model-standards.pdf

Vernon-Dotson, L. J., & Floyd, L. O. (2011). Building leadership capacity via school partnerships and teacher teams. *The Clearing House: A Journal of Educational Strategies, Issues and Ideas, 85*(1), 38–49.

Wenner, J. A., & Campbell, T. (2017). The theoretical and empirical basis of teacher leadership: A review of the literature. *Review of Educational Research, 87*(1), 134–171.

York-Barr, J., & Duke, K. (2004). What do we know about teacher leadership? Findings from two decades of scholarship. *Review of Educational Research, 74*(3), 255–316.

CHAPTER 2

Developing and Supporting Teacher Leaders

"Great leaders do not create followers.
They create more leaders."
~Tom Peters

This chapter will provide an overview of the essential leadership traits school administrators, particularly principals, should ideally possess to foster a culture and climate that values the development and support of teacher leaders.

As stated in the previous chapter, the literature base to support the value of teacher leaders, along with the benefits it provides to students, staffulty, administration, and all levels of stakeholders (parents and community members), is rather robust and spans more than four decades. However, there may still be a general lack of awareness and appreciation for the value or return on investment of dedicating the necessary time and resources to develop effective teacher leaders, as evidenced by Katzenmeyer and Moller (2009) referring to teacher leaders as sleeping giants within our schools.

If you have been working in the PreK-12 system, you are likely aware of the ongoing teacher shortage. Not only are a larger percentage of teachers leaving the profession, but fewer individuals are entering it through teacher preparation programs at colleges and universities. While this is undeniably a complex issue with no single solution, one approach is to enhance the recruitment and retention of qualified teachers by developing and empowering teacher leaders.

Teacher turnover is not only expensive, but it's been associated with an adverse effect on students' academic achievement and decreasing the overall quality of the instructional environment. According to a report by the Learning Policy Institute (2016), "the replacement costs for teachers ranged from $4,366 in a small rural district to nearly $18,000 in a large urban district in 2007 – at a national price tag of $7.3 billion a year. When adjusted for inflation, the national cost of teacher replacement rises to approximately $8.5 billion today" (Podolsky et al., p. 8).

In the article "Environmental Teacher Leadership: Overcoming Barriers Posed by School Culture, School Structure, and the Principal," author Karen Action (2022) states "teacher leaders, despite their significant contributions to schools, are often undervalued and underutilized" (p. 1). Therefore, when school administrators evaluate the costs of investing in professional development to support teacher leaders, it's not a question of "Can we afford it?" but rather "Can we afford not to do this?"

Implementing Teacher Leadership

"There cannot be significant progress within an educational system in which hierarchical control separates managers (school principals) from workers (teachers)" (Katzenmeyer & Moller, 2016, p. 122). Consequently, as the success of any organization is directly tied to the quality of its formal leadership, training and supporting teacher leaders must be a collaborative effort that begins with school and district-level administration.

According to Leithwood and Riehl (2003), "leadership has significant effects on student learning, second only to the effects of the quality of curriculum and teachers' instruction." The authors go on to share the following:

> In sum, school leaders are those persons, occupying various roles in the school, who provide direction and exert influence in order to achieve the school's goals. Formal leaders—those persons in formal positions of authority—are genuine leaders only to the extent that they fulfill these functions. Leadership functions can be carried out in many different ways, depending on the individual leader, the context, and the nature of the goals being pursued. (p. 2)

Accordingly, developing teacher leaders is essential if a school district wants to positively impact student achievement, recruit and retain quality teachers, and foster an effective organizational culture and climate. This effort requires strong, forward-thinking administrators confident in their leadership abilities who are dedicated to prioritizing what's best for students. These formal leaders must possess what I refer to as a leader's superpower: vulnerability. They must be willing to use their authority to *empower others* rather than *wield power over them*, thus creating a positive, impactful, and enduring legacy.

In Chapter 1, I asked if you saw yourself as a leader in your school. I also shared that, based on my personal experience training teachers and teacher leaders at various career stages, most teachers do not see themselves as leaders. According to extensive research by Katzenmeyer and Moller (2016), there are three main reasons why teachers are hesitant to identify as leaders and pursue leadership roles within their schools: School Culture, Lack of Skills, and Traditional Roles (p. 122).

School Culture
Teachers might be hesitant to see themselves as true leaders within their schools, districts, and communities because of the prevailing school culture. Due to various factors, such as current leadership or the culture in which veteran teachers were initially socialized, some teachers have never been encouraged or simply given permission to view themselves as leaders, nor have they worked in environments that value and support this perspective.

An unfortunate consequence of a school culture in which administrators fail to recognize the value of developing and empowering teacher leaders, thus allowing them to stay in the classroom while pursuing additional leadership roles, is that these highly qualified, experienced educators simply leave. "Often, teachers who are motivated to become leaders will leave these unsupportive school cultures and will seek out schools more conducive to their leadership aspirations" (Katzenmeyer & Moller, p. 123).

Lack of Skills
Another reason teachers may not see themselves as leaders in their current instructional roles is that they believe they lack the skills, especially those required to lead adults. "While principals and other leaders are required to learn leadership skills, teachers rarely are engaged in building these skills" (Katzenmeyer & Moller, p. 123).

Although academic programs that prepare principals and other building or district-level administrators provide the appropriate training, leadership is leadership, emphasizing the need for school districts to implement teacher leadership into their ongoing professional development efforts. Subsequent chapters in this book will further explore practical and effective leadership skills that are applicable both inside and outside of the classroom.

Traditional Roles
Finally, teachers can be reluctant to see themselves as leaders or volunteer for teacher leadership roles because, for the most part, teachers are other-centered and don't like to call attention to themselves or stand out. While this is a positive characteristic to have when it comes to supporting students and putting kids first, the downside to this mindset is that it can unnecessarily limit teachers' self-confidence and ability to see themselves serving in other capacities that don't require them to leave the classroom.

Additionally, this mindset may also be reinforced by the more traditional, top-down managerial style historically prevalent in schools. This organizational culture often mirrored that of a rigid classroom, where students were expected to remain seated in rows while the teacher maintained control from the front of the room.

Similarly, this structure extended to the school administration, positioning them at the helm of the school (akin to their own classroom), while teachers, like students, were expected to conform and focus solely on their assigned tasks. Fortunately, this authoritarian style of school leadership is no longer commonplace. However, as with many traditions, lingering remnants of this outdated model may still persist in some schools.

Unfortunately, schools and districts with underdeveloped leadership acumen may impede the training, development, and empowerment of teacher leaders, which ultimately has a negative impact on students. However, the encouraging news is that schools with effective, supportive administrative teams have the potential and are uniquely situated to cultivate a culture and climate conducive to student achievement and school improvement. Additionally, by embracing teacher leadership, these schools can prioritize faculty retention, boost morale, and ultimately enhance overall school performance.

In their article, "Promoting Teacher Leadership: Principal Actions to Promote and Facilitate Teacher Leadership for Enhanced Student Outcomes," Krista Bixler and Marjorie Ceballos (2023) outline the following "Five Actions" that principals can take to support and develop teacher leaders:

- **Action 1:** Create a vision for teacher leadership and embed it in the school culture.
- **Action 2:** Build trusting relationships with teachers.
- **Action 3:** Provide leadership development and mentoring for teachers.
- **Action 4:** Collaborate with teachers on decision making.

- **Action 5:** Provide resources to teacher leaders (p. 24-27).

Action 1: Create a Vision for Teacher Leadership and Embed it in the School Culture

According to Max De Pree, a successful businessman, leadership expert, and author, "the first responsibility of a leader is to define reality" (2004, p. 11). Although there are many ways for a leader to define reality, an integral part of this process is their ability to effectively cast a vision for those they serve. In their book *Simple Truths of Leadership: 52 Ways to Be a Servant Leader and Build Trust*, leadership experts Ken Blanchard and Randy Conley (2022) state "Every great organization has a compelling vision...which includes three elements: your purpose (what business you are in), your picture of the future (where you are going) and your values (what will guide your journey)" (pp. 10-11).

Accordingly, school administrators—especially principals—who hope to awaken the sleeping giant of teacher leadership must establish a compelling vision that inherently integrates developing and supporting teacher leaders into its purpose, future results, and associated values. To further establish teacher leaders as part of their compelling vision, principals should communicate the "primary role of teacher leadership in achieving school improvement goals to all stakeholders through various platforms and channels" (Bixler & Ceballos, 2023, p. 24).

Action 2: Building Trusting Relationships with Teachers

A key component of my personal leadership philosophy is the value of relationships. Leadership is a people business, and while every relationship between a leader and those they serve is nuanced and varied, one thing is clear: effective leaders form relationships and get to know the people they serve. As we will later learn in my Teacher-Leader's Credo, building relationships is not optional.

Trust is another important component of building relationships. Again, I'm reminded of one of Blanchard and Conley's Simple Truths (2022), which states "the opposite of trust is not distrust – it's control" (p. 116). While we could certainly unpack this profound truth at length, the main application is creating a culture that supports and empowers teacher leaders and is built upon positive relationships among principals and teachers that are devoid of an authoritative, micro-managing (controlling) leadership style that can stifle and discourage teachers' growth and development.

Action 3: Provide Leadership Development and Mentoring for Teachers
Although there are instructional standards and frameworks that advocate for developing teacher leaders, intentional leadership training is more commonly found within graduate-level courses and academic programs for principals and superintendents. As a result, to develop teacher leaders, schools must be intentional about not only making it part of their professional development plan, but more importantly, integrating it into their overall culture and climate. Accordingly, this means principals must be well-versed in applicable leadership theories.

It's also important to note that even though a district may select certain teachers to serve as leaders, leadership training should be made available to all staffulty, which further promotes a servant-based culture among the entire team and enhances its overall capacity.

In addition to developing trust and cultivating strong relationships, another essential trait of school administrators aspiring to develop teacher leaders is mentorship. Effective mentors inherently recognize the potential in those they serve and are committed to helping them reach their maximum potential.

Moreover, exemplary leaders and mentors demonstrate selflessness by acknowledging that, at times, what's best for an individual may be neither convenient for the leader nor the organization. It takes a secure and confident leader to understand that a potential consequence of their influence and tutelage is that the person whom they mentored may grow into another job and move on.

Action 4: Collaborate with Teachers on Decision Making

Another skill set required among school administrators capable of implementing teacher leadership programs in their schools is that they must be transparent and willing to collaborate with teachers and other stakeholders. They must be transparent communicators willing to involve teachers in organizational-level decision making. According to Bixler and Ceballos (2023), "collaborative leadership by the principal is critical as it may promote commitment to the school, increased job satisfaction, and [teacher] self-efficacy" (p. 26).

In a report focused on solving the teacher shortage, Anne Podolsky (2016) and her colleagues shared the results of a study that asked over 2,000 current and former teachers in the state of California about factors related to whether or not they chose to remain in the classroom. Among the most prominent factors identified was the quality of relationships among faculty and staff, along with the opportunity to participate in school decision-making.

Leaders who engage with their colleagues and create a culture and climate of collaboration and shared decision-making reflect a form of distributive leadership, which, according to Bennett et al. (2003),

> is not something 'done' by an individual 'to' others or a set of individual actions through which people contribute to a group or organization . . . [it] is a group activity that works through and within relationships, rather than individual action. (p. 3)

Accordingly, this is not a static theoretical framework but more of a philosophical, behavioral-based approach predicated upon seeing, hearing, and valuing every member of the team for the unique perspective and skill set they collectively bring to the organization.

I especially like what my colleague, Dr. Scott Gregory (a current college professor and former school superintendent, principal, and teacher), said about the importance of school administrators possessing the necessary acumen to support not only teacher leadership but any type of research-based, high-impact practice in our schools: "Leadership is not a checkmark item, it's something that is built over time. In short, it's *organically constructed* and *authentically nurtured.*"

Action 5: Provide Resources to Teacher Leaders

Regardless of the organization or business, leaders must effectively allocate resources to those they serve. While time and money are the first resources that come to mind and are undeniably important, effective leaders also recognize there are other resources that contribute to an individual's overall success, satisfaction, and sense of belonging.

Effective resource allocation is especially important and uniquely nuanced for school leaders. Without question, money is not only important but oftentimes scarce in PreK-12 schools. In addition to local, state, and national variables that can influence funding, time is also an invaluable resource, especially for those who work with and are responsible for kids each and every minute of the day.

Despite the challenges posed by limited resources, school leaders must also be aware of the inherent opportunities that effective resource management can provide, such as allocating space for teaching, planning and collaboration, peer coaching, and professional development, to name a few. Accordingly, a school environment in which teacher leaders can be identified, developed, and supported requires principals and other administrators who can effectively support teachers and students through mindful resource allocation.

Developing teacher leaders is essential for enhancing student achievement, recruiting and retaining quality teachers, and fostering a positive organizational culture. However, it requires school administrators with key leadership traits such as vision, trust, mentorship, collaboration, and effective resource management.

"Teacher leaders are not just influencing individual teachers, but also...the entire school, community, and profession" (Wenner & Campbell, 2017, p. 140). Therefore, by embedding teacher leadership into the school culture, building strong relationships, providing leadership development opportunities, involving teachers in decision-making, and allocating resources thoughtfully, school leaders can empower teachers and drive meaningful, sustainable improvements within their schools. The collective effort to develop and support teacher leaders not only benefits the educators themselves but also has a profound impact on the entire school community.

Discussion and Application Questions

1. Reflect on the concept of teacher leadership within your school or district. How does the current culture either support or hinder the development of teacher leaders? Provide specific examples of policies, practices, or attitudes that influence this dynamic.
2. Consider the role of trust and relationships in effective school leadership. How can school administrators build trusting relationships with teachers to foster a culture that supports teacher leadership? What specific actions can you take in your current role to improve trust and collaboration?
3. Analyze the impact of traditional, top-down managerial styles on teacher leadership. How have remnants of this outdated model affected your school's ability to empower teachers as leaders? What changes can be made to shift towards a more collaborative and distributive leadership approach?
4. Discuss the importance of leadership development and mentoring for teachers. What are the key components of an effective leadership development program for teachers in your school or district?
5. Evaluate the allocation of resources in your school or district. Beyond time and money, what other resources are essential for the development and support of teacher leaders?

References

Acton, K. S. (2022). Environmental teacher leadership: Overcoming barriers posed by school culture, school structure, and the principal. *International Journal of Leadership in Education*, 1–21.

Bennett, N., Wise, C., Woods, P. A., & Harvey, J. A. (2003). *Distributed leadership*. National College of School Leadership.

Bixler, K., & Ceballos, M. (2023). Promoting teacher leadership: Principal actions to promote and facilitate teacher leadership for enhanced student outcomes. *Leading & Managing, 29*(1), 21–30.

Blanchard, K., & Conley, R. (2022). *Simple truths of leadership: 52 ways to be a servant leader and build trust*. [Kindle version]. Berrett-Koehler Publishers. https://a.co/d/4Hqb7sz

Katzenmeyer, M., & Moller, G. (2009). *Awakening the sleeping giant: Helping teachers develop as leaders* (3rd ed.). Corwin Press.

Katzenmeyer, M., & Moller, G. (2016). Chapter 13: Understanding teacher leadership. In *Counterpoints* (Vol. 466, pp. 121–136).

Leithwood, K. A., & Riehl, C. (2003). *What we know about successful school leadership*. National College for School Leadership.

Podolsky, A., Kini, T., Bishop, J., & Darling-Hammond, L. (2016). *Solving the teacher shortage: How to attract and retain excellent educators*. Learning Policy Institute.

Wenner, J. A., & Campbell, T. (2017). The theoretical and empirical basis of teacher leadership: A review of the literature. *Review of Educational Research, 87*(1), 134–171.

CHAPTER 3
Roles and Goals of Teacher Leadership

"We are what we repeatedly do. Excellence, therefore, is not an act but a habit."
~Will Durant

Now that we have a better understanding of the value of teacher leadership, how it's defined, and the type of leadership and culture required to support it, you may be asking yourself, "What do teacher leaders actually do?" While this is a great question that will be addressed in this chapter, along with expectations and goals for teacher leaders, I would like to first revisit another important concern associated with teacher leadership.

Teacher Leadership is Not "One More Thing"

A few years ago, I was at a summer meeting with PreK-12 teachers and administrators as we were all preparing for the upcoming academic year. I approached an administrator from a large, well-respected district and said, "What are you doing to develop and support your teacher leaders?" Somewhat taken aback, they replied, "Oh, we don't have time for that since we've already selected our professional development theme for the year. Besides, if we did teacher leadership, our people would see it as adding one more thing to their plates. They're already complaining about next month's back-to-school in-service, so we couldn't possibly add teacher leadership. Maybe we'll look at this for the following year."

While perhaps common among some teachers and administrators, this response reveals an honest lack of knowledge or misunderstanding about the significance of empowering teacher leaders. This type of mindset views teacher leadership as just another meeting or activity that administrators would have to ask their teachers to "do," thus seeing it as an add-on or putting one more thing on their plate.

However, thinking that developing and empowering teacher leaders is just one more thing is akin to refusing to follow your dentist's advice when they tell you to brush and floss regularly. Sure, it's probably a good idea, but do you really have the time to add *one more thing* to your daily routine?

In addition, as discussed in the previous chapter, effective school leaders have the uncanny ability to be vulnerable, set aside their egos, and look into the future, thus positioning the organization to best serve students long-term. In doing so, they are also able to cast a compelling vision, establish expectations, and bring others along with them through developing positive, professional relationships.

Teachers are arguably the most influential people in the school and, if given the opportunity, can become an integral part of the overall administrative leadership team. Therefore, adopting a culture focused on equipping and empowering teachers to serve in various leadership roles is no more something extra on teachers' plates than asking them to be visible in the building as students enter in the morning, requesting they follow the assigned curriculum, or asking them to keep an updated grade book. While admittedly not always easy, some things are simply part of the job and, if done with fidelity and consistency, ultimately help kids and support the school and district as a whole.

Additionally, because great leaders are other-centered and understand they can't do it all, the current demands of overseeing a school or district – external factors aside – are simply too much for one person or even a formal administrative team to handle.

Similar to an athletic team, the head coach and their assistants are certainly necessary and responsible for the organization's success. They must cast a vision, establish a winning culture, build relationships, and set expectations that help the athletes develop and reach their maximum potential. However, the final outcome of the game comes down to how the players can implement the coach's vision and expertise when they perform on the field.

Accordingly, school leaders must understand that adopting a culture that values teacher leadership is a way to expand their own ability to reach into each classroom they oversee and affect students, thus enhancing their overall capacity and adding to the effectiveness and collective potential of their leadership team.

Therefore, all boats rise, and important metrics such as student success, teacher retention, and morale, are positively affected when school administrators realize that the process of developing teacher leaders is not something a school just *does*; it's *who they are*, which is a natural consequence of their culture, values, and beliefs

Teachers are Natural Leaders

Let's now return to the question I asked at the start of this chapter, "What do teacher leaders do?" While we will look at specific roles in which teacher leaders engage, similar to what I said about teacher leadership being part of a school's identity, as opposed to a one-off meeting or workshop, it's important to note that "teachers become leaders in their schools by being respected by their peers, being continuous learners, being approachable, and using group skills and influence to improve the educational practice of their peers" (Podolsky et. al, 2016, p. 11).

While these characteristics can certainly be more thoroughly developed and integrated into a school culture within the context of a formalized teacher leadership program, *all teachers are capable of earning their colleagues' respect, engaging in continuous learning, and influencing others.*

Therefore, I think it's important to emphasize that regardless of whether or not a district implements a formalized teacher leadership program, *all teachers are leaders.*

As a former classroom teacher, I know the inherent value teachers bring to their classrooms, schools, districts, and communities; this helped shape my personal definition of leadership, which is *influence through character, courage, relationships, and service.* Similar to how I analyzed Brené Brown's definition of leadership within the context of being a classroom teacher, I will do the same with my own definition.

Influence

Influence is the foundation upon which all leadership is built; a great leader is the catalyst for helping people move beyond their comfort zone and current abilities in order to achieve things they could not have done on their own. You may recall from your teacher preparation courses studying the Zone of Proximal Development (ZPD), which Lev Vygotsky (1978) defined as "the distance between the actual developmental level as determined by independent problem solving and the level of potential development as determined through problem-solving under adult guidance, or in collaboration with more capable peers" (p. 86).

Although Vygotsky developed the ZPD to refer to learning, as an educator, I believe this is also a fitting concept for all leaders. Think about it. Anyone in a leadership role (teacher, boss, manager, coach, etc.), to some extent, must get a group of people, as individuals and collectively, to move from Point A to Point B in order to accomplish something they would have otherwise been unable to do without the leader's influence.

Accordingly, there are very few professions in which people are inherently required to influence other humans on a *daily, minute-by-minute basis* than classroom teachers. Furthermore, the modalities and environments in which teachers must be influential are not limited to the classroom. If you have taught for any amount of time, I have no doubt that you often think about student supervision. Moreover, if you are an administrator, I would guess you think about student supervision in your sleep!

For example, if there is a potential problem that arises outside of the classroom – especially if it is off school property – I would assume that one of the first questions an administrator must ask is, "Was there supervision?" Why? Because the school is responsible for the wellbeing of students, which requires constant influence. Therefore, if leadership, in a single word, is influence, then teachers are always on the clock influencing others.

Figure 3.1: Leadership Framework

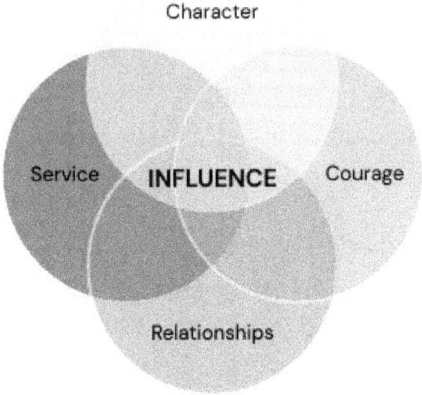

Character

My wife used to teach instrumental music, and I can honestly say she remains one of the best teachers I have ever observed in person. One of the many pieces of teaching advice she shared with me was this: "When working with your students, especially if you are angry, always say *the second thing* that comes to your mind." This was not only great advice but always served as a reminder that as teachers and leaders, we are held to a higher standard and must always display strong character.

How many times have you had to think twice before saying the first thing that came to your mind out of frustration that would not have been in line with your character? How many of you, especially if you teach in a small or rural district, have been hesitant to order an adult beverage with your meal while dining in a local restaurant or worry about what's in your shopping cart while at the grocery store? Why is this? Because leaders are always cognizant of their character and the messages they send to those they serve.

In fact, while this is certainly not legal advice, unlike other professions, teachers are not only held to a higher personal standard but can be disciplined and even terminated if their behavior – inside or outside of the classroom – is deemed significant enough to connect their ability to continue effectively teaching students as a respected authority figure.

Courage

In Chapter 1, I provided an overview of the many ways teachers are courageous by stepping up and being uncomfortable in the service of others. Again, this is not only a non-negotiable characteristic of a great leader but something classroom teachers do daily, oftentimes as part of their instructional practice. For example, consider how you felt in the following scenarios and the extent to which you displayed courage:

- The first time you stood in front of a class to teach your first lesson.
- The first time you had to enforce your classroom rules in a way that significantly upset a student, perhaps resulting in their temporary removal from your class.
- The first time you had to contact a parent or guardian to discuss something uncomfortable or potentially conflict-provoking about their student.
- Making the decision to show up each day to influence kids.

I know there are many other examples of how teachers are consistently courageous on a daily basis to help support their students. Take some time to think about some of the more specific instances in which you show courage, then share these with non-educators, and ask how they would feel doing them. I suspect you will realize that you are uniquely and atypically courageous!

Relationships

I will discuss relationships more in-depth in subsequent chapters, but I'm fairly confident that the notion of developing supportive, professional relationships with your students and colleagues not only attracted you to the teaching profession but might be one of the primary reasons you have chosen to remain in the classroom.

While the success of any organization depends upon the relationships within it, which starts with the leader, as a classroom teacher, you are constantly interacting with your students in a way that underscores and promotes healthy relationships. To a large degree, how you develop and sustain relationships with your students reflects your character and overall teaching philosophy. This further reveals the type of culture, climate, and related core values you have created within your classroom, thus contributing to the extent to which your students feel valued, seen, and heard.

Service

Having worked in the school system and now, more recently, preparing future teachers, I can confidently state that those who are called to the teaching profession are other-centered and have a natural inclination for service, which is a non-negotiable trait among all great leaders. In fact, as chair of a teacher education department, when a college student contacts our office to change their major to education, most of the time, they come from either nursing or social work, thus reinforcing they have been called to one of the *helping-professions* and simply need to determine the best fit.

As a teacher, how many times have you been part of conversations in which the guiding principle was "Let's do what's best for kids" or "We need to put students first"? These are not only great principles but reflect the fact that, to some degree, every adult who works in a school does so to serve students. As we will learn from my Teacher-Leader's Credo, a leader's ability to influence others through displaying a strong character, being courageous, and developing relationships is done *in the service of other people*.

Hopefully, I have impressed upon you that teachers (including you) embody the essence of great leadership. Regardless of whether or not your district intentionally develops and supports teacher leaders, you can still apply the professional and personal development concepts shared in this book to enhance your practice, benefiting your students, colleagues, and other stakeholders.

You can be a successful teacher leader even without formal support, though this may limit your ability to reach your maximum potential. Therefore, let's review some of the roles and frameworks of teacher leadership that schools and districts can implement to further enhance teachers' effectiveness, ensuring success through strong administrative support.

Teacher Leadership Roles

While there are many definitions of teacher leadership, the delineating factor between a teacher leader and a formal or titled school leader/administrator is that the teacher leader's primary role is that of a classroom teacher. Nonetheless, this still enables teacher leaders to influence their colleagues, school leaders, and the broader school community to enhance teaching practices and improve student learning outcomes. In doing so, teacher leaders can support the administrative goals and efforts of their district, expanding their influence outside of their respective classrooms by contributing to a community of learners and sharing responsibility for driving positive educational changes.

In their article, "Solving the Teacher Shortage: How to Attract and Retain Excellent Educators," Anne Podolsky (2016) and her colleagues state the following:

> Teachers in leadership roles work in collaboration with principals and other school administrators by facilitating improvements in instruction and promoting practices among their peers that can lead to improved student learning outcomes. By doing so, they support school leaders in encouraging innovation and creating cultures of success in school. (p. 11)

Although there are many ways teachers can influence others to support outcomes and initiatives within their buildings, districts, and communities, the following is a list of some of the more common roles in which teacher leaders can serve:

- Advisory Board Member (building, district, or state level related to PreK-16 education).
- Assessment Designer
- Career and Technical Education (CTE) Program Instructor
- Clinical Supervisor (CTE or university students)
- Committee Chair
- Content Facilitator
- Cooperating Teacher (university student teachers)
- Curriculum Planner
- Curriculum/Instructional Coach
- Department Chair
- Dual-Credit Instructor
- Lead Teacher
- Mentor Teacher
- Professional Development Facilitator
- Program Coordinator

Look at each of these roles and think about how it requires teachers to lead others. Based on my personal definition, consider the extent to which teachers are asked to positively influence and serve in a way that requires them to build relationships while displaying character and courage. In your experience as an educator, are there other roles you have observed or served in that could be added to this list?

In addition to these roles, it's important to note that a teacher leader can also be defined as the go-to person within their respective buildings—offering advice, mentoring, and support for their students and colleagues.

Teacher Leadership Goals

In their article "Five Goals for Teacher Leadership," Celine Coggins and Kate McGovern (2014) offer a model of five measurable goals that can guide, support, and enhance the implementation and development of teacher leadership programs. These goals are a direct result of their work at Teach Plus, which is an organization "rooted in the belief that leadership opportunities for teachers have a measurable, positive effect on students, schools, and the teaching profession" (p. 16). Having successfully worked with more than 1,000 teachers across the United States, the following will share the goals and associated outcomes that emerged from Coggins and McGovern's work.

Goal 1: Improve Student Outcomes

Among the many benefits of teacher leadership, the most critical is improving student performance, especially within groups that have traditionally been deemed underperforming. In the statistically underperforming schools in which Coggins and McGovern (2014) implemented teacher leadership programs, on average, achievement scores in math and English improved by 16 and 12 points, respectively (pp. 16-17).

Goal 2: Improve the Access of High-Need Students to Effective Teachers

Teacher leaders are especially pivotal in ensuring that high-need students have access to high-quality education. By advocating for an equitable distribution of effective teachers and supporting their peers in challenging environments, teacher leaders advocate for all students.

Coggins and McGovern (2014) found schools that developed and implemented teacher leadership programs, especially those deemed low-performing, also increased their capacity to attract high-performing teachers.

Goal 3: Extend the Careers of Teachers Looking for Growth Opportunities

In order to positively affect students' achievement, growth, and development, schools must be able to attract, support, and retain great teachers, which is perhaps the second most important benefit of empowering teacher leaders.

As part of their work with over 1,000 teachers across the U.S., Coggins and McGovern (2014) found that being given leadership opportunities was cited as one of the primary reasons that over 50% of teachers in their cohorts decided to stay in the classroom (p. 18).

Goal 4: Expand the Influence of Effective Teachers on Their Peers

In Chapter 2, we looked at a few of the reasons teachers either fail to see themselves as leaders or are reluctant to take the initiative to do so. In addition to feeling as though they lack the required leadership skills, the historical top-down managerial style of school leadership may still cause some teachers to be hesitant to lead their peers. Because of this, school administrators must be mindful of this when supporting teacher leaders, which is a result of developing the appropriate culture and climate.

Therefore, Coggins and McGovern (2014) suggest administrators identify teachers who can "take charge without dominating the group" and preferably, display the following skills and characteristics: purpose-driven instructional leaders, skillful facilitators of adult learning, evidence-based decision makers, ongoing learners, and change agents (p. 19).

Goal 5: Ensure a Role for Teachers as Leaders in Policy Decisions Affecting Their Practice

According to Coggins and McGovern (2014), "When teachers have a voice in crafting and implementing policies that affect their daily work—from evaluation reform to testing protocols—

those policies are likely to work better in the classroom" (p. 20). Therefore, in addition to empowering and supporting teacher leaders within their respective buildings, school administrators must also ensure teacher leaders are given the opportunity to contribute to policy decisions at the district, state, and national levels.

Not only do classroom teachers represent the ground floor where the actual teaching, learning, growth, and relationship building occurs with students, but they are also uniquely prepared to help solve problems and suggest equitable, effective, research-based responses to better inform decision-makers at various levels.

Although these five goals are not without limitations, they nonetheless establish a set of clear expectations to which any teacher leadership program should aspire. Additionally, the work presented by Coggins and McGovern underscores and illuminates the many benefits associated with developing and supporting teacher leaders, such as increased student achievement and teacher retention.

Overall, this chapter has hopefully provided a more thorough understanding of the goals and benefits associated with teacher leadership. There are certainly a number of roles teacher leaders can serve that are more formal in nature. However, all teachers are leaders and can strive to meet the needs of students, schools, and communities, guided by the tenets of effective leadership and the Five Goals for Teacher Leadership.

Discussion and Application Questions

1. Based on the definitions and roles discussed in this chapter, how do you see your current or future role as a teacher fitting into the broader framework of teacher leadership?

2. The chapter addresses the misconception that teacher leadership is just one more thing for teachers to do. How can school administrators and existing teacher leaders effectively communicate the true nature and benefits of teacher leadership to their colleagues?

3. Consider the five goals for teacher leadership presented by Coggins and McGovern. Which of these goals do you find most compelling or relevant to your school context, and why? How can you contribute to achieving this goal within your school or district?

4. Reflect on the characteristics of effective leaders discussed in the chapter, such as influence, character, courage, relationships, and service. Identify a specific instance in your teaching career where you demonstrated one of these characteristics. How did it impact your students or colleagues, and what did you learn from the experience?

References

Coggins, C., & McGovern, K. (2014). Five goals for teacher leadership. *Phi Delta Kappan, 95*(7), 15–21.

Podolsky, A., Kini, T., Bishop, J., & Darling-Hammond, L. (2016). *Solving the teacher shortage: How to attract and retain excellent educators.* Learning Policy Institute.

Vygotsky, L. S. (1978). *Mind in society: Development of higher psychological processes.* Harvard University Press.

CHAPTER 4

Teacher Leader Standards: A Model of Success

"Leadership is not about being in charge.
Leadership is about taking care of
those in your charge."
~Simon Sinek

In addition to the various definitions, roles, and goals associated with developing and supporting teacher leaders, there are also a few notable standards that can provide additional guidance for schools and districts as they implement formalized programs. Therefore, the purpose of this chapter will be to provide an overview of some of the prominent frameworks that can guide school administrators looking to support their students by developing teaching leaders.

The Teacher Leader Model Standards

The Teacher Leader Model Standards were initially created by the Teacher Leadership Exploratory Consortium in 2008. This consortium was comprised of teachers and administrators within the PreK-12 system, higher education, and representatives from state education agencies. These standards were developed to recognize and define the critical leadership roles teachers play in contributing to student and school success. Additionally, the standards were developed to promote effective, collaborative teaching practices, improve decision-making at school and district levels, and support a dynamic and evolving teaching profession for the 21st century.

Accordingly, The Teacher Leader Model Standards (2011) should be used as a framework to guide curriculum development, professional development, and the creation of policies within educational institutions. Additionally, they are intended to encourage discussions about the competencies required for teacher leadership and how teacher leaders can complement formal administrative roles, ultimately supporting effective teaching and student success. The Teacher Leader Model Standards are comprised of the following domains:

- **Domain I:** Fostering a Collaborative Culture to Support Educator Development and Student Learning

- **Domain II:** Accessing and Using Research to Improve Practice and Student Learning
- **Domain III:** Promoting Professional Learning for Continuous Improvement
- **Domain IV:** Facilitating Improvement in Instruction and Student Learning
- **Domain V:** Promoting the Use of Assessments and Data for School and District Community
- **Domain VI:** Improving Outreach and Collaboration with Families and Community
- **Domain VII:** Advocating for Student Learning and the Profession (p. 9).

Domain I: Fostering a Collaborative Culture to Support Educator Development and Student Learning

The teacher leader understands the principles of adult learning and knows how to develop a collaborative culture of collective responsibility in the school. The teacher leader uses this knowledge to promote an environment of collegiality, trust, and respect that focuses on continuous improvement in instruction and student learning. (Teacher Leadership Exploratory Consortium, 2011, p. 14)

Domain I exemplifies how administrators can not only expand their influence into each classroom but also empower and work collaboratively with teacher leaders, thus supporting a culture of trust and support. Additionally, it's important to note that one of the functions of this domain is to support collaboration in a way that encourages teacher leaders and administrators to "…solve problems, make decisions, manage conflict, and promote meaningful change" (Teacher Leadership Exploratory Consortium, 2011, p. 14).

Domain II: Accessing and Using Research to Improve Practice and Student Learning

Domain II is centered on teacher leaders' ability to "understand how research creates new knowledge, informs policies and practices, and improves teaching and learning" (Teacher Leadership Exploratory Consortium, 2011, p. 15).

In many ways, this domain supports and encourages teachers to apply the full spectrum of their knowledge and abilities as professional educators. For example, in order to become a licensed classroom teacher, state and national accreditation standards for teacher preparation require teachers to demonstrate a rather robust knowledge of the various fields associated with education, such as educational research, educational psychology, assessment and measurement, classroom management, and social-emotional learning, to name a few.

Therefore, this domain respects and calls upon the inherent professional knowledge and skillset present among all educators. This can include analyzing school and district-level data and making appropriate decisions, supporting new initiatives by researching and analyzing the extent to which they support best practices in the field, and working with community members to effectively communicate supporting rationale for district and schoolwide decisions.

Domain III: Promoting Professional Learning for Continuous Improvement

Function A from Domain III states that "[The teacher leader] collaborates with colleagues and school administrators to plan professional learning that is team-based, job-embedded, sustained over time, aligned with content standards, and linked to school/district improvement goals" (Teacher Leadership Exploratory Consortium, 2011, p. 16).

Consequently, Domain III focuses on how teacher leaders can support a number of school, district, and statewide goals and initiatives by designing, implementing, and overseeing professional development opportunities for their colleagues. Providing teacher-led learning opportunities for all staffulty not only contributes to a sense of ownership and accountability but also enables school administrators to reinforce a culture that values collaboration and respects the professional abilities and opinions of their teachers.

Domain IV: Facilitating Improvement in Instruction and Student Learning
Similar to Domain II, Domain IV also relies upon teachers' eclectic professional skills and knowledge base to collaboratively engage in and model instructional practices that improve student learning. This domain also specifies a few roles in which teacher leaders can serve such as a mentor, coach, team leader, and content facilitator.

In addition to placing an emphasis on emergent technologies to further support student achievement, Domain IV also "Promotes instructional strategies that address issues of diversity and equity in the classroom and ensure that individual student learning needs remain the central focus on instruction" (Teacher Leadership Exploratory Consortium, 2011, p. 17).

Domain V: Promoting the Use of Assessments and Data for School and District Community
Domain V acknowledges that teacher leaders are "knowledgeable about current research on classroom- and school-based data and the design and selection of appropriate formative and summative assessment methods" (Teacher Leadership Exploratory Consortium, 2011, p. 18).

Moreover, this domain calls for all aspects related to data analysis implementation and application to be a collaborative process based on a foundation of trust and critical reflection.

It's worth mentioning that this domain underscores the value professional educators bring to the table when making decisions that bridge the gap between theory and practice. Furthermore, administrators who empower teachers to have a seat at this decision-making table not only demonstrate a culture of respect and collaboration but also build capacity among their team, thus mentoring those who may eventually pursue administrative roles.

Domain VI: Improving Outreach and Collaboration with Families and Community

Domain VI reinforces the notion that it takes a village to educate our students and states "The teacher leader works with colleagues to promote ongoing systematic collaboration with families, community members, business and community leaders, and other stakeholders to improve the educational system and expand opportunities for student learning" (Teacher Leadership Exploratory Consortium, 2011, p. 19).

While the nuances of this approach will vary based on the size, location, and overall demographics of each educational community, this domain nonetheless provides teacher leaders with an opportunity – through various forms of community engagement – to better understand, promote, and support the different backgrounds and educational needs of students and their families.

Additionally, this domain calls on teacher leaders to facilitate their colleagues' "self-examination of their own understandings of community culture and diversity and how they can develop culturally responsive strategies to enrich the educational experience of students..." (Teacher Leadership Exploratory Consortium, 2011, p. 19).

Domain VII: Advocating for Student Learning and the Profession

Domain VII recognizes the obligation and right that all teachers have to advocate for their students and the teaching profession at the state, local, and national levels among various stakeholders. "The Teacher leader...advocate(s) for students' needs and for practices that support effective teaching and increase student learning and serves as an individual of *influence* [emphasis mine] and respect within the school, community, and profession" (Teacher Leadership Exploratory Consortium, 2011, p. 20).

It's important to note that this domain encourages collaboration among colleagues and stakeholders and recognizes that student advocacy will necessarily occur across multiple contexts, both within and outside of the classroom. This also highlights the significance of teachers being advocates for their respective content areas, especially those who teach in classrooms that have traditionally been underfunded or even removed from the school curriculum.

The Teacher Leader Model Standards represent a robust framework that can be used as both a guide and aspirational model for school administrators and their teams who hope to solidify an inclusive and professional culture that values the full spectrum of teachers' abilities to better serve their students, communities, and profession.

InTASC Model Core Teaching Standards

The InTASC Model Core Teaching Standards, developed by the Council of Chief State School Officers (2013) through the Interstate Teacher Assessment and Support Consortium (InTASC), is a commonly used framework among PreK-12 schools, university teacher preparation programs, and state and national accreditation agencies. Designed to ensure that students are college and career-ready, these standards "...

describe what effective teaching that leads to improved student achievement looks like" (p. 3). Additionally, these standards are to "serve as a resource for states, districts, professional organizations, teacher education programs, teachers, and others as they develop policies and programs to prepare, license, support, evaluate, and reward today's teachers" (p. 5).

Developed to be applicable across all content areas and grade levels, there are ten InTASC (2013) standards and related progressions that "describe effective teaching with more specificity than the standards, provide guidance about how practice might be improved, and outline possible professional learning experiences to bring about such improvements" (p. 10). The standards and progressions are grouped into the following four overarching categories:

The Learner and Learning
- Standards/Progressions 1 and 2: Learner Development and Learning Differences
- Standard/Progression 3: Learning Environments

Content Knowledge
- Standard/Progression 4: Content Knowledge
- Standard/Progression 5: Application of Content

Instructional Practice
- Standard/Progression 6: Assessment
- Standard/Progression 7: Planning for Instruction
- Standard/Progression 8: Instructional Strategies

Professional Responsibility
- Standard/Progression 9: Professional Learning and Ethical Practice
- Standard Progression 10: Leadership and Collaboration (Council of Chief State School Officers, 2013, p. 1).

While it is beyond the scope of this chapter and book to analyze and unpack all of the aforementioned standards, it's worth noting that the diverse group of stakeholders tasked with developing a framework to ensure student success and teacher effectiveness recognized the value of leadership.

Accordingly, Standard 10 states that "the teacher seeks appropriate leadership roles and opportunities to take responsibility for student learning, to collaborate with learners, families, colleagues, other school professionals, and community members to ensure learner growth, and to advance the profession" (Council of Chief State School Officers, 2013, p. 45).

To further explain how teachers can serve as leaders, Standard 10 provides the following Progressions:

- "The teacher collaborates with learners, families, colleagues, other school professionals, and community members to ensure learner growth" (Council of Chief State School Officers, 2013, p. 46).
- "The teacher seeks appropriate leadership roles and opportunities to take responsibility for student learning and to advance the profession" (Council of Chief State School Officers, 2013, p. 4).

To provide additional credence to the notion that developing and empowering teacher leaders is undeniably beneficial to the overall support and success of a school district, which ultimately affects student achievement, the following table highlights the connections between the Five Goals for Teacher Leadership (Coggins & McGovern, 2014), presented in Chapter 3, the Teacher Leader Model Standards (Teacher Leadership Exploratory Consortium, 2011), and the various components of

InTASC Standard 10 (Council of Chief State School Officers, 2013).

Table 4.1

Five Goals for Teacher Leadership	Teacher Leader Model Standards	InTASC Standard 10: Leadership and Collaboration
Goal #1: Improve Student Outcomes	Domain IV: Facilitating Improvement in Instruction and Student Learning. Domain V: Promoting the Use of Assessments and Data for School and District Community	10(a) The teacher takes an active role on the instructional team, giving/receiving feedback on practice, examining learner work, analyzing data from multiple sources, and sharing responsibility for decision-making and accountability for each student's learning. 10(c) The teacher engages collaboratively in the schoolwide effort to build a shared vision and supportive culture, identify common goals, and monitor and evaluate progress toward those goals. 10(h) The teacher uses and generates meaningful research on education issues and policies.
Goal #2: Improve the Access of High-Need Students to Effective Teachers	Domain I: Fostering a Collaborative Culture to Support Educator Development and Student Learning. Domain VII: Advocating for Student Learning and the Profession	10(j) The teacher advocates to meet the needs of learners, strengthen the learning environment, and enact system change. 10(k) The teacher takes on leadership roles at the school, district, state, or national level and advocates for learners, the school, the community, and the profession.

Five Goals for Teacher Leadership	Teacher Leader Model Standards	InTASC Standard 10: Leadership and Collaboration
Goal #3: Extend the Careers of Teachers Looking for Growth Opportunities	Domain III: Promoting Professional Learning for Continuous Improvement Domain I: Fostering a Collaborative Culture to Support Educator Development and Student Learning	10(f) The teacher engages in professional learning, contributes to the knowledge and skills of others, and works collaboratively to advance professional practice. 10(i) The teacher seeks appropriate opportunities to model effective practice for colleagues, ead professional learning activities, and serve in other leadership roles.
Goal #4: Expand the Influence of Effective Teachers on Their Peers	Domain I: Fostering a Collaborative Culture to Support Educator Development and Student Learning Domain II: Accessing and Using Research to Improve Practice and Student Learning	10(a) The teacher takes an active role on the instructional team, giving/ receiving feedback on practice, examining learner work, analyzing data from multiple sources, and sharing responsibility for decision-making and accountability for each student's learning. 10(d) The teacher works collaboratively with learners and their families to establish mutual expectations and ongoing communication to support learner development and achievement. 10(n) The teacher knows how to work with other adults and has developed skills in collaborative interaction appropriate for both face-to-face and virtual contexts.

Five Goals for Teacher Leadership	Teacher Leader Model Standards	InTASC Standard 10: Leadership and Collaboration
Goal #5: Ensure a Role for Teachers as Leaders in Policy Decisions Affecting their Practice	Domain VII: Advocating for Student Learning and the Profession Domain VI: Improving Outreach and Collaboration with Families and Community	10(j) The teacher advocates to meet the needs of learners, strengthen the learning environment, and enact system change. 10(k) The teacher takes on leadership roles at the school, district, state, and/or national level and advocates for learners, the school, the community, and the profession.

It's important to note that the two Progressions within InTASC Standard 10 are connected to the Five Goals and the Teacher Leader Model Standards in the table as cross-cutting themes; they are applicable in each category. Additionally, a cursory analysis of each of the table's rows suggests that individuals carrying out these tasks within the school and community must be effective leaders, influencing others through courage, character, relationship, and service.

Teacher leadership significantly contributes to improving educational outcomes, fostering professional development, and advocating for effective teaching practices. Aligning measurable goals for teacher leadership with established standards and frameworks provides a structured pathway for schools and districts to effectively implement and support teacher leadership initiatives.

Discussion and Application Questions

1. Prior to reading this, how familiar were you with the Five Goals for Teacher Leadership? If you were to pick one of these goals to focus on during the current or upcoming school year, which one would it be and why?
2. Reflecting upon the Teacher Leader Model Standards, select one area or Domain that feels pertinent to your specific grade level or content area. How can you support this as a teacher leader?
3. Select at least three components of InTASC Standard 10 that you feel comfortable with as a teacher and would like to model and implement in the future.

References

Coggins, C., & McGovern, K. (2014). Five goals for teacher leadership. *Phi Delta Kappan, 95*(7), 15–21.

Council of Chief State School Officers. (2013). *Interstate Teacher Assessment and Support Consortium InTASC model core teaching standards and learning progressions for teachers 1.0: A resource for ongoing teacher development.*

Teacher Leadership Exploratory Consortium. (2011). *Teacher leader model standards.* https://www.ets.org/content/dam/ets-org/pdfs/patl/patl-teacher-leader-model-standards.pdf

CHAPTER 5
The Teacher-Leader's Credo

―――◄ ►―――

"The first and most important choice a leader makes is the choice to serve, without which one's capacity to lead is severely limited."
~Robert Greenleaf

Before we move on, you may still be thinking to yourself that while all of this teacher leadership stuff sounds really awesome, the reality of your situation is that it won't work because you lack the necessary time, resources, or administrative support. I understand because this is often the concern I hear each time I have the opportunity to train a group of teacher leaders and we come to this point in the process.

However, because I also know what the end result looks like, here is my advice: What follows in this chapter and the rest of the book represents a personal and professional growth journey that has everything to do with you as a classroom teacher and less to do with the type of organizational culture you are in, which certainly includes the quality and dedication of your administration.

In other words, the rest of what you will learn and hopefully apply to your professional practice is 100% up to you. If you happen to be in an environment that supports the formalized development and utilization of teacher leaders, then that's a bonus. You will grow and benefit *because of* your organizational culture and climate.

However, if you feel as though your colleagues, building, or district would be less than receptive to what we learned in the first four chapters, here's my advice: *keep reading*. You are your own Classroom CEO; get better for yourself and your kids *in spite of* your organizational culture. Either way, I am confident that what follows will add value to you and those you serve as you move forward in your career.

Like most educators, I tend to be very eclectic in terms of how I search for ideas and answers, be it for my teaching, research, or professional growth. Accordingly, I have developed my Teacher-Leader's Credo, which represents my own experiences, mistakes, research, and guidance from trusted mentors. Since all teachers are leaders, whether they realize it or not, I have also found that this credo is applicable to leadership roles across a number of situations and professions.

On a daily basis, teachers instinctively display traits that are not only required of some of the top leaders in their industries outside of education but many of these leaders must work hard to acquire these skills. Consequently, I hope you can appreciate the inherent leadership capacity you already possess and display each and every day!

The Teacher-Leader's Credo

1. It's not about me, but it starts with me.
2. I must give up to go up. What got me here won't get me there.
3. I am in the people business, and people are messy. I'm a "people."
4. Other people's irresponsibility will oftentimes become my responsibility.
5. I will never have a perfect group of people, and they will never have a perfect leader.
6. I must be vulnerable. People will see my faults whether I admit them or not.
7. Conflict happens every day, and that's OK!
8. Relationships and influence are not optional.

It's Not About Me, but It Starts with Me

As I have already said multiple times, teachers are other-centered. As with most characteristics and traits, there are pros and cons to being primarily focused on others, especially if it keeps us from establishing healthy boundaries and taking time for ourselves (which we all must do). However, if you have been a teacher for any length of time, you realize that as the Classroom CEO, you show up each and every day to serve others.

It's not about you. You already know your curriculum and would most likely receive 100% on every single one of your assignments. You're an educated adult who knows how to adhere to all of your classroom rules, regulations, and expectations. I would even go so far as to assume that while it's tempting to talk to your colleagues during an in-service, workshop, or meeting, you understand social norms and expectations and pay attention.

As the leader of your classroom, if it were just about you, why would you show up 180-plus days a year when you know all of the things you teach and model for your kids on a daily basis? You show up because others need you. It's not about you; it's about the kids in your room for whom you set the tone, cast the vision, and establish the culture, climate, core values, and expectations of your classroom, thus enabling them to achieve what they otherwise could not.

Although it's not about you, as the leader of your classroom, it does start with you. As a professional educator, you must see "more and before" (as coined by John Maxwell) and possess the delicate and unique skillset that Shulman (1986) referred to as Pedagogical Content Knowledge, which is a perfect blend of knowing your content, your kids, and how to create an environment that enables your students to learn at an appropriate level. As teachers, we all know the importance of starting each day having adequately prepared our lessons that will occur in a classroom environment that, from the first days of school, taught our students the rules, expectations, and consequences necessary for learning to occur.

Finally, realizing it's not about you but starts with you also means we must oftentimes take the high road (and say the *second thing* that comes to mind), be it with a student, colleague, or parent. Yes, it can be frustrating and downright hurtful when another human, regardless of their age, comes at us with negativity. However, as leaders, we must realize it's not about us. The other person's negative attitude is almost always about them, and as the leader, it starts with you showing up, being positive, and leaning into difficult situations.

I Must Give Up to Go Up - What Got Me Here Won't Get Me There
Whether you spend your entire career in the same subject or grade level, move on to administration, or even leave the profession altogether (I hope you don't!), one thing you can count on is change. While it's natural to be somewhat resistant to change, it's necessary for growth and development, both personally and professionally. The process of letting go to grow requires a growth mindset, which is very applicable to teaching and leading. In her book *Mindset: The New Psychology of Success*, Carol Dweck (2016) states the following:

> This growth mindset is based on the belief that your basic qualities are things you can cultivate through your efforts, your strategies, and help from others. Although people may differ in every which way—their initial talents and aptitudes, interests, or temperaments—everyone can change and grow through application and experience (p. 9).

Consider the following scenarios, most of which could be concurrently present within a school building or district at the start of a new academic year and, to varying degrees, require change through a growth mindset.

- Starting a new year with new kids in the same class, grade level, or subject area as the previous year.

- Adopting a new curriculum.
- Teaching a different grade level.
- Teaching in a new classroom or building.
- Serving as a department chair.
- Serving as a curriculum coach.
- Serving as the chair of a district-wide committee.
- Serving as an assistant principal.
- Beginning a new position in the district office.

Overall, those who serve in any type of leadership role must adopt a growth mindset and recognize that what got me here won't get me there. Even if we stay in the same place, we must adapt and change because maintaining the status quo is a failure to grow.

For example, when starting a new school year in the same position as the previous year, the unique dynamics of each group of students require teachers to change and adapt. Relying solely on what worked last year will not suffice; teachers must innovate to meet the new year's challenges and ensure success. In other words, a complete cut-and-paste of what got you here last year will not get you there in terms of being successful in the upcoming school year.

Additionally, when leading outside of your classroom and working with your colleagues and other stakeholders, it's important to acknowledge that the skills, experience, and knowledge base you have as a teacher, while necessary to lead adults, might not be entirely sufficient. This doesn't mean you should shy away from leading your colleagues but instead implies that anytime we step into a new endeavor, we must acknowledge what we don't know and be willing to learn, adjust, and adapt. In fact, one of the guiding principles of the second part of this book is to provide you with the tools to enhance your existing leadership skills.

Figure 5.1: Teacher-Leader's Credo

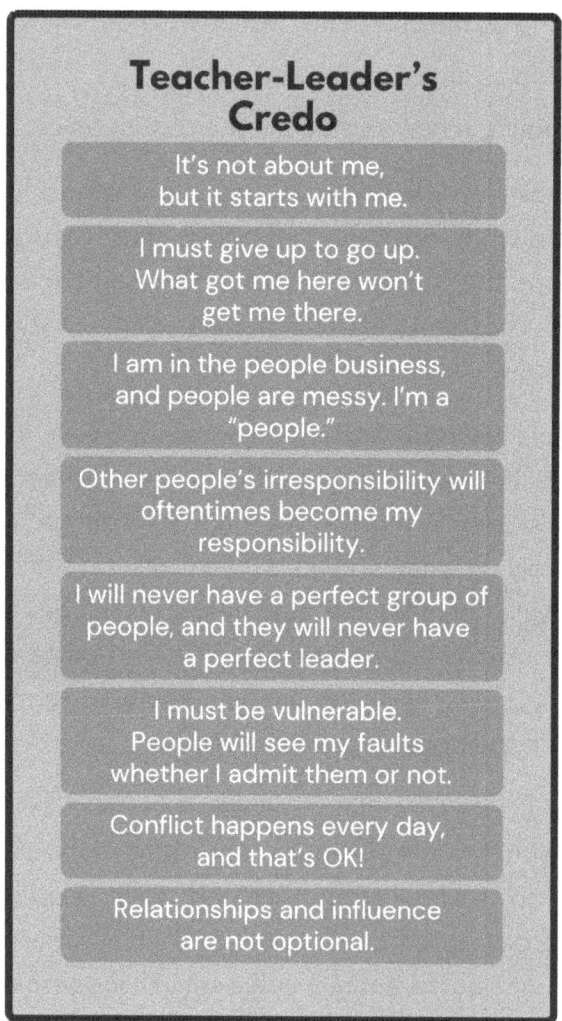

I Am in the People Business, and People Are Messy. I'm a "People"
Serving as a classroom teacher is perhaps the epitome of being in the people business. What other profession works with and is

responsible for other humans (all of whom are minors) on a minute-by-minute basis? For the non-teachers who may beg to differ with this notion, simply tell them some of the "You won't believe this, I can't make this stuff up" stories you have undoubtedly collected over your career. If you are reading this as a preservice teacher, don't worry; you'll have enough to entertain your friends by the end of your first week!

While there is certainly an entertaining side to being in the people business that will make you laugh, teachers also understand the opposite end of the "people spectrum" and have stories and experiences that will make you cry. Once again, on a *daily basis*, teachers are confronted with and must address a multitude of behaviors, both directly and indirectly, that are present in each and every student.

I believe teachers work miracles each day. Think about it. Teachers understand people are messy and come to school with things we can't imagine, and yet, teachers are still able to make personal connections with kids so they can not only learn but feel safe, valued, and respected.

Additionally, as teacher leaders move outside of their classroom to work with and influence their colleagues and other stakeholders, they must also realize they are, first and foremost, serving people. Don't let the bigger bodies fool you; educated adults, with the best of intentions, are still perfectly imperfect people who now bring their personal and professional experiences, burdens, and preconceived notions to the table.

Finally, it's important for every teacher to acknowledge that people are messy, and that includes you; you're a people! As an experienced teacher, I'm sure there have been days you have shown up to school less than excited to teach because of something going on in your personal life. I'm sure there have been times when during a lesson, you have taught many times, your mind is elsewhere, thinking about things that come up in adults' lives. Additionally, I suspect there have been occasions where, after the fact, you regretted how you responded to a student or colleague and acknowledged that it was out of character because of something else going on in your personal or professional life.

Just like your students and colleagues, you're human and bring the best version of yourself to school each day. By recognizing this in yourself and even sharing with your students why you might be off your game some days, you're showing an incredible amount of courage, honesty, and vulnerability, all of which are common traits among great leaders.

Other People's Irresponsibility Will Oftentimes Become My Responsibility

As you may now recognize, a common theme is emerging from this credo: Teachers are natural leaders! Showing up each day to serve others inherently means addressing something you didn't cause or fixing what you didn't break because it's part of the job. Please note that this doesn't mean great leaders lack boundaries and simply fix everything for everyone. However, being in the people business and serving others does require a realization and acceptance that we will be called to be on the other side of another person's irresponsibility and decisions.

I would like to point out, with regard to working with students, the word "irresponsibility" might be a bit harsh for some of the situations teachers address; it may be more appropriate to recognize that other people's *poor choices*, *behaviors*, or *unavoidable, yet inconvenient circumstances*, will become your responsibility. For example, students are not responsible for an overprotective or abrasive parent who emails you and your administration multiple times a day. However, this is something you must still address. Therefore, I'm confident that on a daily basis, many times without realizing it, you display this servant-leader characteristic and respond to issues you didn't create, as indicated in the following scenarios:

- Incomplete or missing assignments
- Undesirable classroom behavior
- Student bullying or other forms of conflict
- Failure to follow instructions
- Coming to class unprepared
- Chronic absenteeism
- Plagiarism or cheating
- Technology issues

Although this is a short, and for some of you, benign list, it nonetheless acknowledges that teachers are the CEO of their classrooms and must display sound character and leadership each and every day by realizing that showing up to serve others means we don't get to choose our inconveniences, surprises, or emergencies.

Likewise, serving others outside of the classroom as a teacher leader also means that, to some degree, you will have to address unavoidable circumstances, poor choices, inconveniences, and, at times, irresponsibility. Additionally, within the context of leading others in your building or district, fixing things might mean you and your colleagues were given a mandate or inherited something that was either neglected or needs to be created for the first time. No one is at fault or to blame, but the task at hand is still robust and will require strong leadership. While not extensive, the following provides a few examples:

- Adopting, implementing, and showing progress for a state-mandated program

- Updating and addressing district-wide curriculum gaps
- Address inconsistencies in teaching and assessment practices among the same grade level.
- Advocating for additional in-service/professional development days to support district and statewide mandates.
- Ensuring building and district professional development programs are relevant and equitable across grades and subject areas.
- Ensuring understanding, application, and consistency for a newly adopted behavior management program for the school or district.

As servant-leaders, teachers must accept that they are frequently called to fix what they didn't break. While this doesn't necessarily cast blame on others, it nonetheless requires influence, courage, and character to adequately address.

I Will Never Have a Perfect Group of People, and They Will Never Have a Perfect Leader

If you have been teaching long enough, think about the best class you ever taught. What made it this way? What were some of the desirable characteristics that still stand out? Does this mean that particular group of students was perfect, always behaved, everyone received 100% on each assignment, nobody's parent called or emailed, no one ever forgot their homework, missed school, and so on? Moreover, does this mean you were a perfect teacher during that school year, and, like the students, you really didn't have to plan lessons, manage the classroom, or grade assignments because those students were just that perfect?

Although I'm sure your best group of kids, or best overall school year, was truly one for the books, I also know that as long as both you and your students were human, there were still unavoidable issues, problems, and conflicts. In fact, for some of you, the best group of kids you had, which may have also defined your best year of teaching, might have been precisely because things were less than perfect, and you were able to overcome them and end the year better than you started it!

All great leaders realize that perfection, certainly as it pertains to other people, is largely a myth. In fact, leaders who are ineffective, controlling, or downright toxic will hold the pursuit of perfection over people's heads precisely because it's unrealistic, thus employing a method to control the culture and narrative of the organization. Accordingly, these are what I call "Yeahbut" leaders. No matter how successful or happy you are, they always bring up a Yeahbut as a means of control.

For example, within a classroom setting, if a student were to tell their teacher they received a 98% on a difficult test, the Yeahbut leader would say, "Yeah, but there's still 2 percent you didn't know, so don't get too excited."

In another scenario, if a fourth-grade teacher and their class received the top score for their state reading assessments, the Yeahbut principal might say, "Yeah, but as a school, we still had some areas of concern, so we need to worry about that."

Being an effective teacher leader means acknowledging you will never have a perfect group of students, and they will never have a perfect teacher (that's you). While this is not an excuse to take it easy, give everyone a pass, and not pursue excellence, it's a sound reminder that, as humans, we all need a reasonable amount of grace, which, at times, includes the benefit of the doubt, thus reminding us to keep our expectations high but still reasonable – for our students and ourselves.

In addition, realizing that we will never have to work with and for perfect people, and they will also never have a perfect colleague or employee (again, that's us), helps us lead both laterally and up. For example, when working with your colleagues and other stakeholders in a leadership role, you are leading *laterally* in terms of a typical organization chart. You are not their boss, they are not your employees, but you must nonetheless influence them to accomplish a task. If you are like me and can sometimes be competitive and impatient, remembering that no one is perfect is an effective way to maintain perspective and treat others in a way that is positive and adds value to them.

Likewise, this same perspective on perfection, or lack thereof, also helps when we are *leading up*, which occurs when you are working alongside or supporting your bosses or administration. It's natural if this is a somewhat new concept to you, especially if you have only worked in more traditional, top-down, managerial-style schools. However, it's important to realize that just as students must recognize their teachers are human and make mistakes, the same is true among teachers and administrators.

Remember that your principal must answer to those above them, such as the superintendent and school board, along with addressing conflict you can neither imagine nor would want to deal with most days. Accordingly, always strive to be a good leader to your leaders by extending them grace, providing the benefit of the doubt, and remembering they are not perfect.

I Must Be Vulnerable. People Will See My Faults Whether I Admit Them or Not

Vulnerability is a leader's superpower. As I shared in a previous chapter, my view has been significantly influenced by the work of best-selling author Brené Brown, primarily built upon two of her quotes:

- "Vulnerability sounds like truth and feels like courage. Truth and courage aren't always comfortable, but they're never weakness" (Brown, 2012, p. 37).
- "Vulnerability is not winning or losing. It's having the courage to show up when you can't control the outcome" (Brown, 2018, p. 19).

As teachers, we all know that students – especially Kindergarteners and middle schoolers – can see our faults and be brutally honest despite our best efforts to hide them. In fact, this teacher truth has now gone viral, and if you search some of the more popular social media platforms, you will find teachers who routinely share their lists of "Things my students have said to me!"

Granted, there are certainly times when students say things to teachers that are untrue or cross the line, and they are made aware of this and may experience a consequence. However, the fact that teachers show up each day to work with humans whose prefrontal cortex – the part of the brain responsible for regulating thoughts, emotions, and actions – is not yet developed is the definition of being a vulnerable and courageous leader, especially when you can't control the outcome!

Therefore, as a teacher, you are uniquely qualified to understand the power of being vulnerable. Acknowledging your faults, within reason, not only makes you more human to your students but also sends the message that they are not expected to be perfect either. Overall, being vulnerable with those you influence sends the message that it's safe to be yourself, to take chances, be unsuccessful, and try again. While perhaps not in the literal sense of the word in terms of final grades, your vulnerability clearly tells your students that your classroom is a *safe place to fail*.

For example, consider how you have felt or responded to leaders who are courageous and emotionally evolved enough to display vulnerability to those they lead. Did this make you feel controlled and less committed to the organization, or did it empower you to take chances and push a few boundaries because you knew it was safe to fail? Regardless of what the outcome, goal, or product is within the organization (teaching kids, making widgets, or getting good grades and passing to the next class), individuals will always accomplish more when their leaders are willing to be vulnerable, thus creating a safe place to fail.

While you may be fairly comfortable with the notion of showing vulnerability and acknowledging your faults to your students, it can nonetheless be difficult to do when working with and leading other adults, such as your peers. If this is true for you, don't worry. There is a natural, built-in dynamic within classrooms that places the teacher at the top of the organization chart, thus giving them more flexibility and grace to be vulnerable. However, when working with your peers or *leading laterally*, the stakes are understandably higher because we want to be successful and appear competent. It's one thing for our students to judge us; it's entirely different when it comes to our peers; we can't assign them a low grade, give them detention, or call their parents!

Nonetheless, leadership is leadership, and regardless of whom you are serving, vulnerability is still your superpower. Be honest, be transparent, show your faults, and let others know they are free to do the same. Whether you are contributing to or leading a group of teachers or stakeholders, having the courage to be vulnerable will undoubtedly pay dividends by empowering those you serve to be themselves, take chances, and strive for excellence, all while having permission to fall short of perfection.

Conflict Happens Every Day, and That's OK!
All right, let's be honest. Most normal human beings neither enjoy nor do they actually want to engage in most forms of conflict, especially when it involves directly communicating with or confronting another person. In fact, I would be a bit skeptical about the character of someone who actually sets out each day to cause or engage in conflict.

Furthermore, in my own experience as a leader, as well as training current and future leaders in both PreK-12 and higher education, without question, if there is one thing that almost universally keeps people from pursuing formal, titled leadership positions, it's the notion of conflict. As we will see in a subsequent chapter, it is possible to learn how to positively and effectively engage in conflict, even if we are never completely comfortable with it.

However, because I have the unique perspective of having served as a public-school teacher along with training leaders, I can confidently state that whether you realize it or not, you are already more adequately equipped to effectively and humanely address conflict than the majority of the population, which includes individuals who may already be serving in high-level, leadership positions. In fact, most teacher preparation programs offer an entire class based on the principle of addressing conflict: classroom management.

I have often said, somewhat in jest but also with an element of truth, that everything I needed to learn about addressing conflict as a university leader, I learned as a public school teacher. While I have certainly addressed my fair share of uncomfortable, high-stakes conflicts during my time as a department chair, some of which have resulted in having to discipline or terminate others, I have yet to step into a situation with the full-blown intensity that only an angry parent can bring!

As a teacher, you understand that in the life of every leader, some form of conflict happens every day, and that's OK! In fact, the difference between a day with or without conflict is akin to how you feel when your students are making an acceptable level of noise, as opposed to how you feel when, all of a sudden, it gets quiet; *that's when you worry*!

Although we will go into addressing conflict more in-depth later in the book, it's important to realize and acknowledge that, as a teacher, you step into conflict each and every day, which is yet another sign of a great leader. Furthermore, you are also more equipped than you may realize to address conflict among your peers. And don't let the college degrees and teaching awards fool you, when you get a group of passionate educators together, albeit with the best of intentions to support kids, some type of conflict will happen. However, just like your own classroom, start by casting the vision, norms, and expectations and realize you can positively, constructively, and humanely address problems and concerns.

Relationships and Influence Are Not Optional

If you have spent your entire professional career in PreK-12 schools, you might be surprised to learn there are actually people out there, some of whom end up being promoted into significant, high-paying leadership roles in large corporations, who either lack the desire or the ability to establish and maintain a healthy working relationship with those they serve. Yes, these leaders are also in the people business, but they, along with the organizations they oversee, will never reach their full potential without establishing a culture, climate, and core values built on sound relationships. You simply cannot influence those you don't know.

I'm fairly confident that one of the main reasons you went into teaching was to influence and build relationships with your students. As you know, a kid is more likely to work with and for you if they first know you care, which is a result of a sound relationship. Additionally, I would suspect the same is true of you with respect to your own leaders and administration; it's important that they know and invest in you.

We are all different, and, as a result, you will work with and lead those with whom you have very little in common or perhaps don't particularly like. Let's be honest; the same could be said of your students and their parents. Nonetheless, it's possible to step up, display integrity, and be the leader they need by showing them respect and ensuring that, as individuals, they are valued, seen, and heard.

Overall, I hope that through sharing the Teacher-Leader's Credo, you have a better understanding and appreciation of how teachers, on a daily basis, must display traits that are inherently those of effective leaders both in and outside of education.

Discussion and Application Questions

1. After reading this chapter, do you feel more empowered as a leader? Why or why not?

2. Share the Teacher-Leader's Credo with a school administrator to determine the extent to which it is also relevant to their leadership role.

3. Look at each element of the Teacher-Leader's Credo and give yourself a letter grade for your current comfort level. What can you do to improve on the elements in which you received less than a grade of B?

References

Brown, B. (2018). *Dare to lead: Brave work. Tough conversations. Whole hearts.* [Kindle version]. Random House. https://a.co/d/5C2eoSj

Brown, B. (2012). *Daring greatly: How the courage to be vulnerable transforms the way we live, love, parent, and lead* (1st ed.). Gotham Books.

Dweck, C. S. (2016). *Mindset: The new psychology of success.* [Kindle version]. Ballantine Books. https://a.co/d/5NbX7db

Shulman, L. S. (1986). Those who understand: Knowledge growth in teaching. *Educational Researcher, 15*(2), 4–14.

CHAPTER 6
Developing Your Mission Statement

—◄►—

"A personal mission statement becomes the DNA
for every other decision we make."
~Stephen Covey

When you develop and plan your lessons and related assessments, I'm sure you know the value of starting with the end in mind. For example, best practice suggests we should know what we ultimately want our students to understand, do, create, and accomplish at the end of an instructional unit and then work backward, designing daily activities and supporting assignments aligned to these objectives.

As a classroom teacher, regardless of how many years you have been teaching, I have no doubt that the last thing you would do when designing an instructional unit would be to simply turn to page one in the book and plan "day one, activity one" and go from there, eventually realizing you should probably give the students a few assignments and perhaps a final, summative evaluation.

Just like we begin planning our lessons knowing the end result, which provides us with a roadmap to inform decisions as we work towards our goals, the same is true for our professional lives. Regardless of whether your goal is to remain in the classroom, move into more formalized teacher leadership roles, or become an administrator, developing your professional mission statement provides you with your own guide or curriculum, which is articulated with and represents your professional self.

Therefore, the key objective of this chapter is to come alongside and guide you through a process that will enable you to develop your Professional Educator Mission Statement. To accomplish this, you will need to be an active participant, taking notes and reflecting on the process, which is akin to completing the formative assessments within an instructional unit.

Before we begin, I would like to mention a few key points. First of all, like any mission statement, please know that what you create is a fluid work in progress. Granted, there are some foundational aspects of who you are and what you believe that will always be present in your mission statement; these will stay with you as you gain experience and progress throughout your career. However, at the same time, it's important to realize that some aspects of your mission statement can and will change to reflect the nuances and growth that come with experience.

In addition, the focus of your mission statement will be from the standpoint of a professional educator, and there are a few reasons for this. First of all, since one of the main objectives of this book is to uncover and develop the inherent leadership abilities within all teachers, it's important to establish a baseline or foundational philosophy that addresses why you initially entered the profession along with the reasons and guiding principles that support your decision to stay.

Doing so will also reveal that while major corporations worldwide spend significant time and money developing and hopefully living out their mission statements, as a teacher, you've been doing this from your first day in a classroom! You know why you do what you do and for whom you show up every day.

Moreover, if you assume more teacher leadership roles or transition into an administrative position, you will likely still consider yourself a teacher, whether you serve as a curriculum coach, dean of students, principal, or in another capacity. Developing a mission statement from the perspective of a classroom teacher further clarifies and reinforces your commitment to being a professional educator, even as you serve students from a different role within the school.

Finally, creating your mission statement from the perspective of a professional educator will enhance your understanding of the process. This insight will enable you to replicate it in the future, regardless of your position. As a leader, you can also guide others through this process, whether individually or as a group (e.g., department, school, district), to develop an organizational mission statement. In the end, a professional mission statement can serve as a north star, helping you make decisions that are in line with your character, values, and beliefs.

Professional Educator Mission Statement Development

To provide an overview of the process in which we are about to collaboratively engage, it's important to ensure you have enough time to commit to each of the three steps, which correspond to three spheres of influence.

Figure 6.1: Spheres of Influence

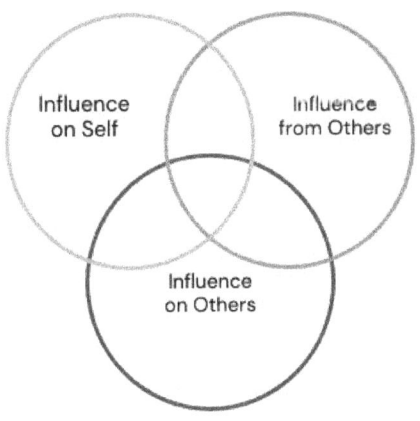

In addition, please be sure to respond to each of the questions and create a list of keywords; focus on the _actions_, _phrases_, _characteristics_, and overall _descriptions_ that best exemplify the character and behavior of the people represented in the questions and prompts. These will be used to build the phrases in your mission statement as in this example:

*"As a professional educator, my purpose is to <u>positively inspire and motivate students</u> **(Phrase 1 response)** with <u>care, energy, and empathy</u> **(Phrase 2 response)** so that <u>they thrive and grow in a safe but challenging environment</u>* **(Phrase 3 response)**."

Keep an open mind and realize that your first draft isn't your final draft because, like your own professional development, your mission statement is a continuous work in progress.

Step 1: I Can Influence Myself

Before we can lead others, we must be able to lead ourselves. To complete this step, you will need to think about your passions, talents, gifts, and overall purpose. Therefore, take some time to reflect upon and answer the following questions.

Step 1. Question 1: What do you like to do?

If you could do anything for a day and truly be in your happy place or zone, what would you do? This doesn't need to include teaching or any other type of job, and while it should be more realistic than not (i.e., don't say you would win the lottery or buy an island) it can nonetheless be somewhat aspirational. For example, while it might not be realistic today or tomorrow, indicating that part of your happy place is a vacation destination is completely acceptable.

Once you have determined what you would do on your free day (don't worry, taking this day off doesn't mean leaving sub plans or twice the work when you get back), relax, play out the scene in your mind and focus on the following questions:

- What are you doing?
- How are you doing this?
- Why do you enjoy this? What about this specifically gives you joy and fulfillment?

- How does this make you feel?

Take some time to focus on the keywords and phrases for each of the questions, ensuring that you could adequately paint this picture if you were describing it to someone else.

As a final question, if someone else were to observe you in your zone doing the things you like, how would they describe you? What would they see, and why would they know, without a doubt, you are doing what you truly enjoy? Again, take time to write down the words you believe someone else would use to answer this question.

Step 1. Question 2: What are your strengths?

I'm going to give you permission to do something that, as a teacher, might feel uncomfortable and perhaps arrogant: Toot your own horn! Yes, it's OK. You are an exceptionally talented and skilled professional who can do things the majority of the population cannot. So, while it may feel a bit awkward to brag about yourself, it's necessary and healthy to realize that, like every other person in the world, you have a unique set of talents and gifts only you can share. Therefore, answer the following questions:

- What are you good at? What do you enjoy doing?
- In what areas are you naturally intuitive?
- In what areas have you excelled or continue to excel?
- What would your best friend or a close family member say are your top strengths and talents?

While these questions might not elicit the same types of answers as the previous questions, you can still focus on the actions and overall characteristics that are inherently a part of your strengths and talents. For example, if you identified that you are naturally intuitive at building things, what skills and characteristics emerge once you unpack what is required to carry out that task?

Step 1. Question 3: What are you passionate about?

In addition to identifying what you like to do along with recognizing your personal gifts and talents, it's also important to reflect upon things you are passionate about. Similar to the previous two questions, while it's understandable if you happen to list things that relate to teaching, it's not required. You have permission to list anything for which you have a strong passion. To help you identify this better, the following questions might be helpful:

- What consumes you? What is always on your mind or catches your attention?
- What keeps you up or wakes you up at night?

The last question isn't designed to be negative but instead focuses on the fact that some of the things that either keep us up or wake us up at night are because, again, we tend to be consumed by these thoughts, and it can be hard to calm our minds.

To further assist you in capturing your ideas, you might find it helpful to use the following table, focusing on the key actions, phrases, and characteristics.

Table 6.1: Step 1 Questions

I Can Influence Myself		
What do you like to do?	What are your strengths?	What are you passionate about?

Step 2: I Have Been Influenced by Others

As the name implies, this step enables us to further analyze those who have influenced our lives, both personally and professionally. To both reinforce Step 1 and introduce Step 2, I would like to share a quote by Adam Grant, a well-known speaker, best-selling author, and professor of Organizational Psychology, who said:

> To understand people's passions, ask what they love to do. To know their values, find out who they look up to – and why. The virtues we cherish in others are a window into what we hold most dear. The strengths we admire are a mirror that reflects who we aspire to become (X, n.d.).

I have had the opportunity to teach this process of developing either an individual or corporate mission statement to a number of people both in and outside of education, and without question, when we get to this step – even among non-educators – the lasting impact and legacy of teachers is almost universal. Actually, I have yet to teach or present this step without taking a short bird walk to discuss the enduring value our teachers had on our lives. Accordingly, please know that what you do matters, and as a result, there are or will be other humans who will mention you, smile, and think of you fondly when asked about their most influential teachers!

Getting back to Adam Grant's quote (see, I always take a bird walk here), you were asked about what you love to do (your free day) in Step 1 in order to uncover things you are passionate about. Additionally, to determine how this relates to your values, some of which were influenced by others, Step 2 will focus on your teachers and other influential people.

Step 2. Question 1: Who was your favorite teacher?

If we're being honest, most of us probably became a teacher, to some extent, because we had one or more great teachers in our lives. Keep in mind that this question can also refer to a favorite coach who, even if they weren't your classroom teacher, was nonetheless an integral part of the school culture and your overall educational development. Therefore, as you reflect upon this person, consider the following, once again taking note of the keywords, actions, and attributes:

- Why was this person your favorite?
- How would you describe this person? What would someone see if they were to observe them in their element?
- What did this person do?
- How did this person behave?
- How would you describe this person's character?
- What was this person passionate about?
- How did this person make you and others feel?
- What did this person enable you and others to do or become?
- Do you still repeat some of this person's sayings or hear them in your head?

I would like to specifically call your attention to two questions, starting with the one about this person's passion. Were you able to share what they were passionate about? If so, I would also guess that while you enjoyed, or at least didn't have a problem with what they taught, it was their passion for teaching and working with kids that made their class enjoyable. You knew they wanted to be there each day. This aligns with the Teacher-Leader's Credo in that people can always see our faults but also our passion. In addition, it takes vulnerability to conduct ourselves in a way that shares our passion – something that can be personal – with others.

How did you respond to the final question? Do you still, as an adult, say things this person said, applying what they taught you, or hear their voice in your head, perhaps when you are either up against adversity or celebrating success? If so, this further underscores the true influence teachers have in all of our lives.

Now, repeat this process (Step 2. Question 1) two more times, and instead of reflecting on your favorite teacher, think about another influential person (non-teacher) in your life, answering the same questions. This could be anyone from a family member to a boss to a piano teacher.

Finally, identify someone who currently serves as a close friend or mentor and answer the questions a third time. As a reminder, to help the overall process, be sure to write down the keywords and phrases that emerge related to each individual.

Table 6.2: Step 2 Questions

I Have Been Influenced By Others		
Favorite Teacher or Coach	Influential Persion (not a teacher)	Friend or Mentor (current or potential)

Step 3: I Can Influence Others

Now that we have worked through identifying and unpacking how you can influence yourself along with being influenced by others, the final step is to tie it all together and recognize how you, like all great teachers/leaders, can and will influence others on a daily basis. Remember, you will be the person someone thinks about when they are asked about their favorite, most influential teacher.

Step 3. Question 1: How do the people you serve know you are a passionate professional?
Let's be honest. It's an unfortunate reality that there are a few teachers out there who are less than passionate about their job. And while some may actually verbalize their discontent with others, their actions speak the loudest. In fact, most students, regardless of their age, can tell if their teacher isn't passionate about their job and doesn't want to be there. It's true that we all have bad days where we may appear to be less than engaged in our work. However, given enough time, our true passion, or lack thereof, is undeniably evident to those we serve.

To answer this question, take some time to reflect upon how people know you are passionate about your job. What are some of your daily habits that ensure others will know that you like what you do? Overall, what are some of the intentional actions and observable characteristics you employ each day so your students and colleagues know you are a passionate professional?

Step 3: Question 2: How do you want to make those you serve feel? What do you hope to enable them to do, accomplish, or become?
When you identified your favorite teacher in Step 2, it's possible that while you may not have initially enjoyed what they were teaching, who they were as a person – their character, passion, integrity – was more influential and impactful than their content. If your favorite teacher taught you in middle school or high school, it's likely you may have come to enjoy their subject area precisely because of how they made you feel and what

you were able to accomplish. (Recall Vygotsky's Zone of Proximal Development from Chapter 3.)

Therefore, think about how and what you hope your students feel as a result of being in your class on a daily basis. If you were to ask your students as they entered your room how they felt, what would they say? How would they respond if you asked them the same question at the end of the class period or school day? Additionally, as a leader in your school, district, and community, how do you make your colleagues and stakeholders feel? What would they say before and after interacting with you?

As a professional educator, what do you hope to enable your students to do, accomplish, or become? Again, thinking about your favorite teacher, I would suspect that the majority of their students didn't go on to become teachers who all taught the exact same subject. Accordingly, what were you able to accomplish and ultimately become as a result of being in this teacher's class? Likewise, what are your goals and aspirations for your own students? Moreover, as a teacher leader, what do you hope to enable your colleagues to achieve or become, in part, due to your collegiality and influence?

Step 3. Question 3: *If someone were to observe you, what would they see, and how would they feel?*

Depending upon a few factors, such as how long you have been teaching, the quality and depth of your mentoring, or the brutal honesty of your students, your answers to this may vary. Nonetheless, take time to step back and reflect upon what someone would see, how they would describe you, and how they would feel as a neutral observer in your classroom.

How would this person, whom you didn't know was observing you, describe your actions or respond to the question, "What does this person do as a teacher?" How would they feel after having been in your classroom? Please note that while this is similar to what you were asked in the previous question, it's designed to address these questions from a neutral observer with whom you would not have direct interaction.

Finally, think about how a colleague or stakeholder would describe you if they were to observe you leading a meeting, serving on a committee, or interacting in your community. How would they describe what you were doing, how you were doing it, and how it made them feel?

Table 6.3: Step Three Questions

I Can Influence Others		
How do the people you serve know you are a passionate person?	How do you want to make those you serve feel? What do hope to enable them to do accomplish and become?	If someone were to observe you, what would they see, and how would they feel?

Preparing to Write Your Mission Statement

Now that you have completed the process of identifying how you can influence yourself, how others have influenced you, and how you will (or continue to) influence those you serve, the final activity will bring it all together to help you write your professional educator mission statement. To accomplish this, synthesize your responses from the previous three steps, finding the core themes that unite your reflections. Use Table 6.4 to compile your responses.

1. Analyze Actions
   - Review all your responses and create a list of key action words that represent your passions, talents, and the actions of your influences.
   - *Now, identify three to five common themes from this list of actions.* These themes will be the verbs in Phrase 1: My Purpose.
2. Analyze Character & Descriptions
   - Review your responses and list all characteristics and descriptive words (adjectives) that portray your character and the character of your key influences.
   - *Next, identify three to five common themes from this list of descriptions.* These themes will describe how you have been influenced by others as well as how you hope to influence and affect those you serve.
3. Analyze Feel, Accomplish, Become
   - Review your responses and list all the desired impacts – what you or others *felt, accomplished*, or *became* – as a result of the three spheres of influence.
   - *Finally, identify three to five common themes from this list of impacts.* These themes will be the desired Impact on Others in Phrase 3.

Table 6.4: Summary of Responses

Influences	Actions	Characteristics & Descriptions	Feel, Accomplish, Become
Step 1 **Influence Myself**			

Influences	Actions	Characteristics & Descriptions	Feel, Accomplish, Become
Step 2 Influence From Others			
Step 3 Influence On Others			
Common Themes			

Before moving on, please reflect upon the Spheres of Influence (Figure 6.1), a Venn diagram representation of the process we have just gone through to help you create your Professional Educator Mission Statement. While I realize that, as teachers, we all appreciate a good Venn diagram, I actually believe this is the best way to visually represent what you have just developed.

Figure 6.1: Spheres of Influence

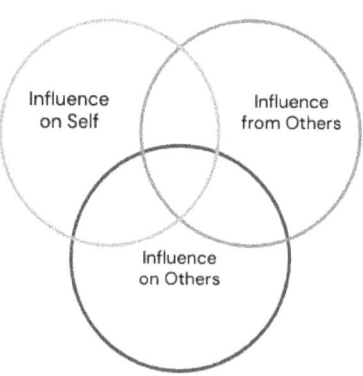

As professional educators (and as individuals), we are the sum of our life experiences and influences, which is what we ultimately have to share with our own students. In fact, this is true of any profession that involves serving others, not the least of which is leadership, both inside and outside of education. Therefore, please realize that the sweet spot of this diagram – who you are and how you influence others – is a fluid and dynamic process, which can change based upon how we grow as individuals along with our own influences and how we choose to influence others.

Writing Your Mission Statement

Now that we have gone through the formative tasks within this developmental process, it's time to complete the final, summative task of writing your Professional Educator Mission Statement. To accomplish this, you will need to have access to all of your responses to the previous questions and tables within this chapter. Please ensure you have enough time to commit to this final step.

Phrase 1: My Purpose

The final statement will be comprised of three phrases that correspond to the steps you will take here, the first of which relates to your overall purpose. To complete the following phrase, focus primarily on the Actions you listed in Table 6.4. Ideally, this should not contain more than three actions or verbs.

> As a professional educator, my (goal, mission, purpose, passion) is to_____.

Phrase 2: How I Will Embody My Purpose

In this phase, focus on the behaviors you will display and the character with which you will embody your purpose, passion, and goals to influence those whom you serve. Reviewing the

Characteristics & Descriptions column in Table 6.4 might be helpful.

> *I will display and embody my (goal, mission, purpose, passion) by displaying_____.*

Phrase 3: Impact on Others

To complete the third phrase, think about the impact your actions and character will have on others and what it will enable them to do, accomplish, and become. Refer to the Feel, Accomplish, Become column in Table 6.4. One thing to note is that while this will most likely refer to the impact you will have on your students, subsequent versions of this statement can be changed to reflect others as you move into different professional roles.

> *I will embody my goals, mission, purpose, and passion of Phrase 1, by displaying the characteristics/descriptions of Phrase 2 in order to, or so that those I serve will (do, see, feel, accomplish, and become) _____.*

As an additional teacher's note, as you may know, the best way to operationalize an instructional objective is to place "in order to" or "so that" after it since, in the English language, this requires a verb. For example, as a former Spanish teacher, the objective of "study the past tense" is neither exciting nor does it actually tell us what or why we are doing it. However, by simply changing this to "study the past tense *in order to tell your friend what you did last weekend,*" we now have a clear indication of why we are doing this and how we can use it.

Finally, to narrow this down and make it more specific, you can convert your responses to the three Phrases into this format:

> As a professional educator, my (goal, mission,
> purpose, passion) is to **(Phrase 1 response)**,
> (with/how/by) **(Phrase 2 response)**,
> (in order to/so that) **(Phrase 3 response)**.

Finally, keep in mind that to further simplify your mission statement, you could start it with "To (Phrase 1)..." since it implies that it's your goal, mission, and purpose as a professional educator.

Sample Statement

As an example of how it all ties together, let's look at the following mission statement and then unpack it within the framework we just followed:

"As a professional educator, my purpose is to positively inspire and motivate students with care, energy, and empathy so that they thrive and grow in a safe but challenging environment." (As previously mentioned, this statement could be reduced and simplified to start as *"To positively inspire and motivate students..."*)

Here is how this statement was developed, based on the three phrases:

> **Phrase 1: "As a professional educator, my purpose Is to positively motivate and inspire."**

This aligns with the educator's overall goal, purpose, or mission, as supported by the influential actions they identified in previous steps.

> **Phrase 2: "I will enact and embody my purpose with care, energy, and empathy."**

Here, we can see how this educator was influenced by those who displayed strong character and took actions to care for and show empathy while also being energetic.

> **Phrase 3: "I will embody the goals, mission, and purpose of Phrase 1, along with displaying the characteristics of Phrase 2 so that the students I serve can thrive and grow in a safe but challenging environment."**

The final part of this mission statement operationalizes what this will enable the students to do, accomplish, or become, along with the environment in which it will occur.

Your Professional Educator Mission Statement

For the final step, complete the following prompt with your Professional Educator Mission Statement. Keep in mind this is not only something that can and should evolve as you progress through your career, but it can also guide you, providing direction as you make decisions related to your many roles as a teacher or even your overall career trajectory.

Professional Educator Mission Statement

As a professional educator...

_____

_____

_____

I encourage you to review your mission statement or invite a friend or colleague to do so. While it's certainly clear that a teacher wrote it, consider whether it indicates the grade level, age group, or content area you teach. From my experience, many educators develop their mission statements in a way that doesn't specify whether they teach elementary, middle school, or high school.

What is evident, however, is their dedication to teaching kids, with the grade level or content area simply being the vehicle through which they accomplish this. Rarely, if ever, has this process produced a mission statement of "Teach kids Spanish so they can learn vocabulary words and conjugate verbs." As a professional educator, you impact your students daily, extending beyond the curriculum to leave a lasting legacy in their lives.

At the beginning of the chapter, I related this process to designing an instructional unit in which we always start with the end in mind and work backward, developing tasks that will introduce and reinforce the main objectives and also equip students to be successful on the final, summative assessment. Much like a well-designed unit, while the final assessment or project is certainly important, it's what we learn along the way that is oftentimes the most educational.

Accordingly, while I hope you were able to develop an impactful and applicable mission statement, I also hope going through the process of identifying your passion, purpose, related influences, and how you hope to influence your own students was a rewarding and rejuvenating experience.

Keep this mission statement close as you continue to read this book. Many of the personal and professional leadership concepts we will explore align with and are guided by this statement, thus reflecting who you are and your aspirations for those you serve.

Discussion & Application Questions

1. Other than creating the final mission statement, what were three other *aha* moments or takeaways you had that will impact how you influence others?

2. Your mission statement can serve as a guide, especially during tough times. Therefore, think about some difficult situations you have experienced in your career, or perhaps you are going through at the moment, and test drive your mission statement. To what extent does this help you make the correct decision, even though it might be difficult and unpopular?

3. As a result of developing your mission statement, discuss one area you discovered was a strength you might not have realized. How can you build upon this strength as you continue to influence your students, colleagues, and others?

References

X (Formerly Twitter). (n.d.). *x.com*. https://x.com/AdamMGrant/status/1493587618705162245

CHAPTER 7

Leadership is a Day Job

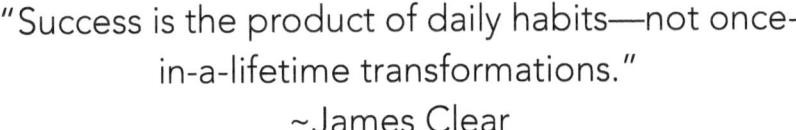

"Success is the product of daily habits—not once-in-a-lifetime transformations."
~James Clear

Since the skills required of an effective teacher resemble many of the competencies required of any great leader, you have hopefully come to appreciate and uncover the many talents you already possess for positively influencing others. I also hope you have been able to build upon your natural leadership acumen and further equip and enhance your leadership development, regardless of whether you remain in the classroom, assume more teacher leadership roles, or move into administration.

As a classroom teacher, you already understand the importance of your daily agenda. Almost every minute of your schedule is accounted for, whether teaching, supervising students, or preparing to do so. In fact, as the chair of a teacher education department, when I hire faculty members directly from the PreK-12 schools, part of my onboarding message is to let them know that their daily schedule and commitments will look different.

For example, they are free to use the restroom whenever they want, they can take more than seven minutes to eat lunch (and can even leave campus to do so), and they will never be asked to supervise the parking lot before and after classes. (For those who come directly from teaching high school, I also tell them that they will never be asked or voluntold to chaperone the prom!)

Most importantly, I assure our new colleagues that outside of the times they are teaching, holding office hours, or in a required meeting or event, they are not only free to leave the campus whenever they want, but they are also not required to check in and out with our administrative assistant.

I mention this because classroom teachers instinctively understand the importance of a consistent, daily schedule along with possessing the discipline to carry it out. It's not hyperbole to suggest teachers are so busy serving others that most days, they have little time to eat lunch or use the restroom. Because of this, I believe very few professions require the intentional minute-by-minute planning and supervision required of teachers.

Consider the amount of work it takes to prepare substitute plans to be gone for one day and then the additional work to catch up upon returning. Ask non-teachers if, to take a day off, they must plan and account for the entire day and do so in a way that leaves detailed instructions to keep other humans engaged.

While I am confident you already understand and implement some of the concepts we will discuss in this chapter, having taught this material to PreK-12 teachers, I know it will nonetheless add value to you and those you serve and further enhance your leadership development.

As the title of this chapter suggests, leadership is a day job. You might wonder how this can be true when teachers work beyond typical school hours, attending school functions, coaching sports, sponsoring events, or preparing for classes on evenings and weekends. Indeed, teachers have more than a day job and work tirelessly outside the traditional workday. However, regardless of the number of hours worked, time of day, or days of the week, the extent to which leaders can positively affect others is based on their attitude, actions, habits, and routines each and every day.

Daily, Not In a Day

In his book, *The 21 Irrefutable Laws of Leadership,* best-selling author and leadership expert John Maxwell (2007) presents the "Law of Process," stating that "leadership is developed daily, not in a day" (p. 23). Maxwell explains that you can tell a great deal about a person's priorities, goals, and future trajectory by looking at their daily agenda: "See what a person is doing every day, day after day, and you'll know who that person is and what [they] are becoming" (p. 25). This is an important concept for leaders everywhere, and teachers naturally understand and apply it as part of their professional practice.

Consider what your daily habits and routines would look like if I observed you each day. What would I see? What are you enabling others to do? Based on Maxwell's definition, there's a good chance I would see you engage in a set of consistent, disciplined habits that build upon one another to make certain your students feel safe and valued and are put in an environment that gives them the best chance to be successful. (Recall in Chapter 6 how we focused on what you wanted others to see, feel, or become as part of your mission statement.)

Designing an effective instructional unit that enables students to learn new concepts requires daily habits and routines. Think about something you teach every year that tends to be challenging for most students. Instead of trying to teach them everything in one day, you must intentionally work over a number of days to help them grasp the content.

This is why, like most teachers, you may feel stressed or anxious when there's an unexpected change to the schedule and you lose instructional time; you know exactly how many days you need to prepare your students adequately. Like all great leaders, you intentionally plan each day to serve others, understanding that productive days build upon one another and, like money, accumulate interest and grow in value.

A Leader's Daily Five

Many years ago, when I was in college preparing to be a teacher, one of my more influential professors would always remind us to ask ourselves – daily – if we would have enjoyed being a student in our class that day. While I accepted this was undoubtedly great advice, as I progressed through my career, I realized the significance of asking this question daily to ensure I showed up as the best version of myself.

As I started to learn more about leadership and transitioned into a titled position as a department chair in a university, I was once again able to draw upon my experiences as a classroom teacher to develop my leadership abilities to best serve others, based upon that one question.

By now, you have hopefully come to realize that my goal as a writer is to be a colleague and mentor and do so in a way that is conversational and, at times, vulnerable. Therefore, I would like to acknowledge that as a native Nebraskan, I may be a bit biased by the source of what I'm about to share. However, I know from experience it can be helpful to all levels of leaders, especially you as a teacher leader.

In his book, *Dream Like a Champion: Wins, Losses, and Leadership the Nebraska Volleyball Way*, John Cook (2018), arguably one of the most successful collegiate volleyball coaches in the sport's history (4 national championships, 8 national finals, 12 national semifinal appearances, 15 conference championships, career winning percentage of .834), shares that each day, he asks himself the following questions:

- "Who needs me today?"
- "Would I be chosen again for this job?"
- "Would I want to be coached by me?" (p. 97).

When I first read this, I immediately thought about the advice I was given about asking myself each day if I would enjoy being a student in my own class. At the time, I was already serving as a department chair, so I reflected upon how, based on Coach Cook's model, I could also ask myself daily questions to help me become a better servant leader.

What emerged is a series of questions I refer to as the Leader's Daily Five. Asking myself these questions each day has been helpful to me and those I have taught and mentored; I am confident they will also be valuable to you and those you serve:

1. Would I want to be my leader today?
2. Whom am I serving today?
3. Am I willing to be uncomfortable for others?
4. Who needs me today?
5. Am I improving others by improving myself?

Before we move on and analyze each of these questions, I hope you have realized that the words "teacher" and "leader" are synonymous. In addition, I encourage you to review these questions from the perspective of both a teacher and a teacher leader working with your colleagues and other stakeholders. If you are considering pursuing an administrative job, consider these questions from that point of view.

Would I Want to Be My Leader Today?

This is a powerful question to ask ourselves at the beginning and end of each day because we are all human, and some days are better than others. Teaching and adulting at the same time can be hard work. And while we are certainly entitled to our feelings and emotions, as leaders, we are held to a higher standard because "It is not about me, but it starts with me."

Therefore, as you start your day, based on your feelings and overall attitude, ask yourself if you would want to be your leader. This does not mean you must always be perfect and ignore your feelings. Asking yourself this question will help you recognize and address thoughts and feelings that may have gone unnoticed.

In addition, whether it is at the end of each class period or the end of the day when you have time to yourself, ask if you would have enjoyed being your leader (your teacher, colleague, etc.) that day. Keep in mind that, at times, it is acceptable to say "no." This shows your vulnerability and enables you to reflect and grow. Sometimes, simply acknowledging an action, choice, feeling, or behavior can make us more aware of when we might be likely to repeat it.

Figure 7.1: A Leader's Daily Five

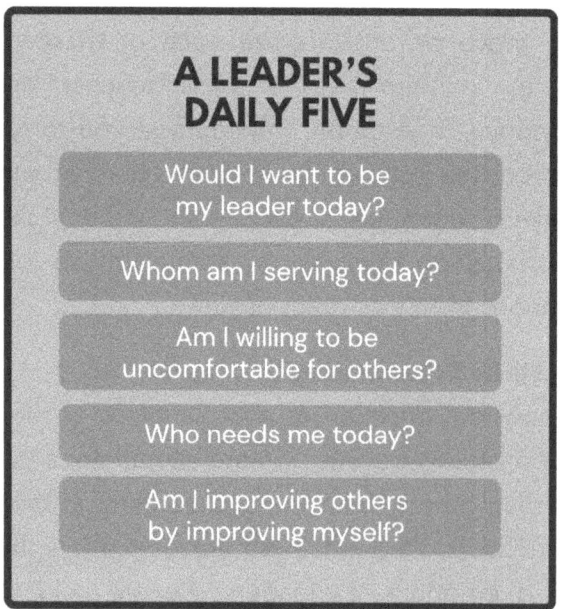

Whom Am I Serving Today?

It is a recurring theme in this book that teachers are naturally other-centered and, as a result, understand their job is to positively influence and serve others daily. As I said previously, you already know your content and would probably receive 100% as a student in your class. You show up for the students; they don't show up for you. Nonetheless, it's human nature to have some days where we get tired, maybe selfish or entitled, and would rather serve ourselves. Remember, you're in the people business, and you're a people too!

Asking yourself, "Whom am I serving today?" along with identifying where your attitude is on the spectrum of "I deserve" to "I'm here to serve," can be very powerful and transformative. Like your students, you're not perfect and may come to school with things that throw you off your teaching game. However, if asking yourself and calling attention to whom you feel like serving each day moves the needle towards the I'm-here-to-serve end of the spectrum, you've been successful.

Am I Willing to Be Uncomfortable for Others?

When I train leaders outside of PreK-12 education, their most consistent concern, or even fear, about stepping into a leadership position is addressing conflict. I understand this because it's uncomfortable for most people. However, leaders are in the people business, which means they must be willing to be uncomfortable in the service of others. Simply put, leadership requires courage.

Let's revisit Brené Brown's (2018) definition, in which she describes a leader as "anyone who takes responsibility for finding the potential in people and processes, and who has the courage to develop that potential" (p. 4). As a teacher who is constantly serving others and influencing their behavior, perhaps without realizing it, you display courage each day and lean into situations that most people would consider uncomfortable. Put another way, you conduct yourself as a courageous leader.

However, just because you do this each day doesn't mean it's easy and free of anxiety. It's called hard work for a reason. Asking yourself if you're willing to be uncomfortable for others can serve as a gentle yet consistent reminder that, as a leader and professional educator, this is a daily expectation of which you are fully capable.

Who Needs Me Today?
I'm sure you start each day with the realization that many people will need you, most of whom are your students. In addition, other people may need you each day, such as your colleagues or students' parents. Nevertheless, while many people rely on you daily, the exact composition of these people and their particular needs will vary. The ways in which your students need you can change daily as well. In addition, as leaders, we often don't know who needs us and why until we show up in the morning.

A student who rarely asks questions or needs extra help might suddenly require your attention and support for a personal reason that upsets them. A parent who usually doesn't contact you may have sent a lengthy email listing all the reasons your classroom rules and expectations shouldn't apply to their child. Your colleague might have a minor emergency during your planning period and need you to supervise their classroom for a few minutes.

While it's not always possible to anticipate the specific ways in which people will need you each day, simply recognizing this fact by asking, "Who needs me today?" can help remove some of the initial surprise or even frustration. In the life of an effective leader, no two days are the same in terms of who needs you and why. Asking this question also serves as a reminder that leaders must develop relationships with those they serve, supported by interacting with people differently based on their daily needs.

Am I Improving Others by Improving Myself?

There's a good chance you are reading this book as a form of professional development, realizing that doing so will make you a better leader and positively impact those you serve, such as students and colleagues. As a natural servant leader, you're improving yourself so you can also improve others.

While engaging in traditional forms of professional development, such as attending workshops, conferences, and taking college classes, is valuable, I consider this macro-level development; formal events within a set period of time characterize it. Since leadership is a day job, effective leaders should also focus on micro-level development, which is informal and more personalized, such as reading (daily quotes, blogs, books), listening to a podcast, or watching videos that provide small, yet effective takeaways you can apply to your personal or professional life.

Whether it's through asking the Leader's Daily Five or carrying out other tasks that enable you to positively and consistently affect those you serve, leadership is a day job predicated upon our daily choices, interactions, and behaviors. Therefore, to further support your continued growth and development, it's also important to recognize the impact of our daily habits.

Daily H.A.B.I.T.S.

According to James Clear (2018), author of the *New York Times* best-selling book *Atomic Habits*, "Few things can have a more powerful impact on your life than improving your daily habits" (p. 27). Further emphasizing that leadership is a day job, Clear goes on to say the following:

"If you want to predict where you'll end up in life, all you have to do is follow the curve of tiny gains or tiny losses and see how your daily choices will compound ten or twenty years down the line" (p. 19).

Although Clear's statements are directed toward individuals, they are also relevant to classes, groups, teams, and organizations. Think about a time that you and your students were successful and, like an instructional unit, work backward and unpack the achievement into daily habits (choices, behaviors, actions), representing the tiny gains you achieved along the way.

Additionally, think about a time when you were part of a team or organization that either failed to meet expectations or had a negative culture. Can you identify a series of daily habits representing the tiny losses that, over time, compounded and contributed to the final result?

As a guide to further assist leaders with recognizing how their daily habits – each decision, interaction, behavior, and thought – stack upon one another and ultimately account for our individual and collective success, I created the following acronym for HABITS. This serves as a resource for leaders to be mindful of their daily habits to optimize how they influence others.

- **H**ere and Now
- **A**ttitude and Affirmations
- **B**elief in Others
- **I**ntentional

- **T**alk and Treat
- **S**elf-Care and Development

Here and Now

As leaders responsible for influencing others daily, we must always recognize that the only place we can actually be influential is in the present: here and now. Granted, great leaders can see ahead to cast and support a vision, along with learning from past behaviors, but the only space in which they can personify their values and promote a positive culture is in the present.

As you go through each day, I encourage you to focus your choices, actions, interactions, and behaviors in the here and now, ensuring your daily habits align with your character, enabling you to serve others in the moment. Similar to how it's helpful to say the second thing that comes to mind when interacting with our students – especially if we are upset – I'm reminded of a quote frequently, albeit incorrectly, attributed to Victor Frankl: "Between stimulus and response there is a space. In that space is our power to choose our response. In our response lies our growth and our freedom" ("Alleged Quote," n.d.).

This quote has implications for all aspects of our lives. However, within the context of serving others, it can also be helpful to realize that while the temporary nature of something in the here and now might seem inconsequential, our responses can leave a long-term impact.

Therefore, it's helpful to make it a habit to ask ourselves how important something will be tomorrow, next week, next month, or in one year. How we choose to respond and behave today – especially to those we serve and influence – can and will matter and impact them long-term, beyond today, next week, or next month.

Attitude and Affirmation

Attitude can be defined as a "manner, disposition, feeling, position...with regard to a person or thing; tendency or orientation, especially of the mind" ("Attitude Definition & Meaning," n.d.). As I'm sure you have told your students many times, while we can't control what happens to us, we can control how we respond based on our attitude. We are given 365 opportunities each year to start our day by deciding to be positive, which, as shown by its definition, encompasses all aspects of our feelings and behaviors about ourselves and others.

In addition to choosing our attitude each day, we can also positively affect ourselves and others through affirmation, which is "The assertion that something exists or is true" ("Affirmation Definition & Meaning," n.d.). Have you ever been positively or negatively affected by another person's affirmation or lack thereof? For instance, when you selected your most influential teacher, I'm fairly confident that, in part, you did so because they made it a habit to have a positive attitude, which included affirming that they saw and valued you as both a person and a student.

The question of "Who needs me today?" from the Leader's Daily Five aligns closely with choosing a positive attitude and affirming others daily. Teachers interact with and influence more people in one day than most other professions. You understand the impact your attitude and words of affirmation can have on that one kid who, despite their outward behavior, truly needs you that day. The kid for whom your words of encouragement and affirmation – saying "I see you," "I value you," and "You matter" – might be the only time they hear those words.

Belief In Others

I had the opportunity to attend a leadership conference, and one of the many excellent speakers was John U. Bacon, an award-winning author, public speaker, and professor. He also used to coach hockey, and in his book, *Let Them Lead: Unexpected Lessons in Leadership from America's Worst High School Hockey Team*, (2021) Bacon describes the unlikely, inspirational journey of the Ann Arbor Huron High School River Rats hockey team, which he miraculously turned around.

Within three years of inheriting a team that didn't win a game the season before he arrived, they were ranked fourth in the state and 53rd nationally, thus surpassing 940, or 95 percent, of all high school hockey teams in the country (Bacon, 2021, loc. 148).

In his third year, before a regional final against Trenton, one of the top teams in the nation, Bacon called his friend and legendary hockey coach Herb Brooks for advice. Brooks coached the 1980 United States hockey team that won gold, famously defeating Russia in the "Miracle on Ice" game.

Brooks' advice was as follows: "Above all, you gotta believe. If you don't, nothing is possible. But if you do, anything is possible" (Bacon, 2021, loc. 158). (If you're curious, the River Rats lost that game 3-2, having lost to Trenton 13-2 the previous year. The next year, in Bacon's fourth season, they defeated Trenton 4-3, marking the school's first victory over them in 20 years.)

I share this story because it shows the transformative power of our beliefs. Similar to how we can choose our attitude and actions to affirm others daily, great leaders are intentional about demonstrating their belief in others. As a teacher, I'm sure you understand the power of letting your students know you believe in them.

Oftentimes, knowing someone believes in us is precisely what it takes to achieve what we otherwise thought was impossible. I suspect you have experienced this on both sides of the desk as a student and now a teacher. It's also likely you understand the value of a boss or leader having the courage to express their belief in you and others daily, thus offering guidance, motivation, and hope.

Figure 7.2 A Leader's Daily Habits

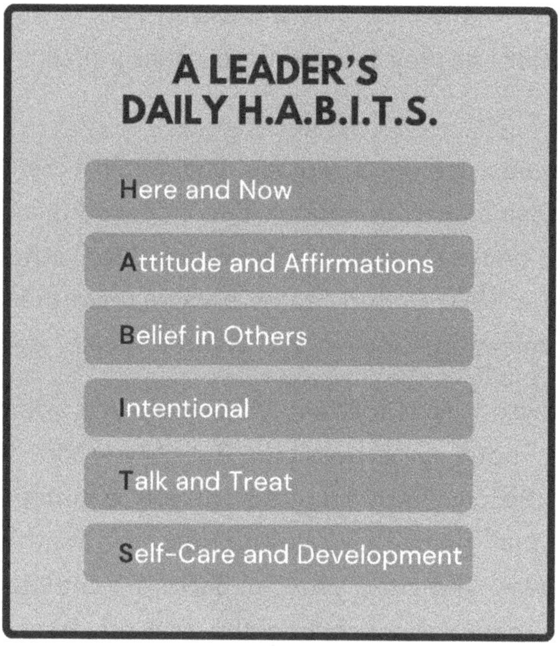

A LEADER'S DAILY H.A.B.I.T.S.

- **H**ere and Now
- **A**ttitude and Affirmations
- **B**elief in Others
- **I**ntentional
- **T**alk and Treat
- **S**elf-Care and Development

Intentional

What does "being intentional" mean to you? Think about your typical day and identify five intentional actions you routinely perform. According to Merriam-Webster, "intention" is "what one intends to do or bring about" and "a determination to act in a certain way" ("Intention Definition & Meaning," n.d.) Our intentions and related thoughts, actions, words, and behaviors are conscious decisions.

Additionally, intentional actions are typically clear in our minds. We know what, how, and why we're doing them. At the beginning of each school year, you are likely to communicate, practice, and intentionally reinforce your classroom rules, procedures, and expectations. This is conveyed to your students with clarity, leaving no confusion about the classroom's what, how, and why, along with the associated consequences. Ideally, the same clarity exists within your building or district; everyone understands why and for whom they show up each day and how they will conduct themselves.

Whether it's a teacher, a district superintendent, or the president of a bank, intentional leaders know their purpose and carry out daily habits and routines with great clarity. Each day, interaction by interaction, these leaders act on purpose, influencing and adding value to others through their attitudes, affirmations, decisions, and behaviors. Regardless of whether you are leading students, colleagues, or community members, make it a daily habit to be intentional about how you positively impact others.

Talk and Treat
Part of being intentional about how we interact with others relates to how we talk to them. As a teacher, how do you actually influence your students so they will make choices and modify their behavior in a way that aligns with your rules, expectations, and curricular objectives?

Whether they're in a classroom or a boardroom, leaders can't make people do anything. Think about some of your toughest students. You know very well – especially in a PreK-12 setting working with minors – that you can't force students to do something they don't want to do, and you certainly can't use physical force. Instead, it's your words, actions, and how you treat them that ultimately influence their choices and subsequent behavior.

Leaders must also make a daily decision to be intentional about how they treat others. While this doesn't mean being a pushover who avoids conflict and making tough decisions, it does require treating people with kindness, extending them grace, and most of the time, the benefit of the doubt. Think about how your most influential teachers treated others. Being kind and considerate wasn't just something they did occasionally; it was part of their daily routine. It was just who they were. Our words matter and contribute to the sum of how we treat people and make them feel. As a leader held to a higher standard each day, be intentional about how you talk to and treat others, including yourself!

Self-Care and Development

Have you ever considered who you talk to the most in a day? You might think it's a family member, a colleague, or a friend, but the real answer is "you." We converse with ourselves more than anyone else. The voice in our head is our own, and how we talk to ourselves reflects how we feel about and treat ourselves. This, in turn, impacts our self-care and personal development.

Imagine starting your day by telling yourself that the world is terrible and everyone is out to get you. This negative mindset can manifest in your interactions with others, affecting how you talk to and treat them. Over time, these tiny losses accumulate, leading to a negative attitude and making you less pleasant to be around. Remember, as leaders, people notice our faults whether we admit them or not, and this includes a poor attitude.

On the other hand, if you begin each day by telling yourself that you are capable, choosing positivity, and speaking words of gratitude and affirmation, the cumulative effect can be profound. This positive mindset can make you a more grateful and enjoyable person to be around. The tiny gains from this daily choice will positively influence your personal growth and development.

While positive self-talk is crucial, nurturing your physical and emotional well-being through other means is equally important. Although I'm not an expert in personal health care, I recognize the value of dedicating time each day to activities that promote your physical and emotional wellness. Consider incorporating regular exercise into your routine. Make this an intentional part of your daily schedule, or at minimum, engage in these activities three to four times a week. Possible activities include:

- Walking
- Jogging
- Weightlifting
- Yoga
- Any physical activity you enjoy

In addition, try to schedule at least one activity each day that fulfills you emotionally. This might include:

- Reading for pleasure
- Listening to music
- Practicing mindfulness or meditation
- Engaging in a hobby you enjoy

Making a deliberate, daily choice to engage in these habits can significantly contribute to your overall self-care and development, personally and professionally. Remember, it's difficult to influence others if we don't take the time to recharge ourselves. By consistently practicing these self-care habits, you invest in your well-being and enhance your capacity to effectively lead and support others.

Credo, Daily Five, H.A.B.I.T.S, and Principles

As we come to the end of this chapter, you hopefully have a more thorough understanding of the importance of a leader's daily habits. As a classroom teacher, it's likely you already engage in some intentional, daily behaviors that directly or indirectly support your students and their overall success.

Similar to how we help our students internalize, recall, and apply information through targeted questions and subsequent reflection, effective leaders must also ask themselves daily questions in order to remain true to their overall purpose while also ensuring continued personal and professional growth.

I define leadership and its associated principles as influence through character, courage, relationships, and service. In addition, I believe it's important for all leaders to accept and lean into the Teacher-Leader's Credo, which provides useful reminders about the realities of leading other people. Therefore, to provide an overview and framework of the relatedness of the predominate principles and frameworks presented to this point, please review Table 7.1 and consider the following questions:

Table 7.1 Credo, Daily Five, H.A.B.I.T.S, and Principles

Teacher-Leader's Credo	Leader's Daily Five	H.A.B.I.T.S.	Leadership Principles
It's not about me, but it starts with me.	Would I want to be my leader today?	Here and Now	Character
I must give up to go up. What got me here won't get me there.	Am I improving others by improving myself?	Self-Care and Development	Service
I am in the people business, and people are messy. I'm a "people."	Whom am I serving?	Belief in Others	Relationships
Other people's irresponsibility will oftentimes become my responsibility.	Who needs me today?	Intentional	Service
I will never have a perfect group of people, and they will never have a perfect leader.	Am I willing to be uncomfortable for others?	Attitude and Affirmations	Character
I must be vulnerable. People will see my faults whether I admit them or not.	Would I want to be my leader today?	Talk and Treat	Courage
Conflict happens every day, and that's OK.	Am I willing to be uncomfortable for others?	Here and Now	Courage
Relationships and influence are not optional.	Whom am I serving?	Talk and Treat	Relationships

- Are there additional components of the Leader's Daily Five, H.A.B.I.T.S., or Leadership Principles that you would add to each of these boxes that also align with the Teacher-Leader's Credo?
- Look at the "Conflict happens every day, and that's OK" row, and think about a time when you had to address some type of conflict with a student, colleague, or another person. Review the Daily Five, H.A.B.I.T.S., and Leadership Principles. To what extent did you follow these? If you did, were they helpful? If you didn't follow them, would they have been helpful and affected the end result?
- Think about a possible scenario that you are currently facing and apply the information from this table. Do you think this will be helpful?

Leadership, at any level and regardless of title, is challenging. Even with the best of intentions, no one is perfect. It's unrealistic to hit the mark every day, successfully answer all the questions, carry out each habit, and display all the principles of effective leadership. Sometimes, our daily attempts and pursuit of excellence, in themselves, are victories, indicating our continued efforts to positively affect those we serve by improving ourselves as leaders. Remember, leadership is a day job.

Discussion and Application Questions

1. As a teacher, were you aware that you naturally carry out the leadership-is-a-day-job mindset? Why or why not?
2. Reflect on the Leader's Daily Five. Think of a time in the past when this might have been helpful. Could you use this to address something you are currently facing?
3. What is one thing you could commit to doing to support self-care and development?

References

"Affirmation Definition & Meaning." (n.d.). *Dictionary.com.* https://www.dictionary.com/browse/affirmation

"Alleged Quote." (n.d.). *VFI / Alleged Quote.* https://www.viktorfrankl.org/quote_stimulus.html

"Attitude Definition & Meaning." (n.d.). *Dictionary.com.* https://www.dictionary.com/browse/attitude

Bacon, J. U. (2021). *Let them lead: Unexpected lessons in leadership from America's worst high school hockey team.* [Kindle version]. Houghton Mifflin Harcourt. https://a.co/d/8OxzJED

Brown, B. (2018). *Dare to lead: Brave work. Tough conversations. Whole hearts.* [Kindle version]. Random House. https://a.co/d/5C2eoSj

Clear, J. (2018). *Atomic habits: Tiny changes, remarkable results: An easy & proven way to build good habits & break bad ones.* Avery, an imprint of Penguin Random House.

Cook, J., & Vogel, B. (2018). *Dream like a champion: Wins, losses, and leadership the Nebraska volleyball way.* [Kindle version]. University of Nebraska Press. https://a.co/d/a787B4Q

"Intention Definition & Meaning." (n.d.). *Merriam-Webster.* https://www.merriam-webster.com/dictionary/intention

CHAPTER 8

The Power of Relationships

―――◄ ►―――

"Kids don't learn from people they don't like."
~Rita Pierson

Developing and sustaining relationships, a required trait among great leaders, can be difficult and doesn't come easy for everyone. However, classroom teachers have a significant advantage over other professions, as forming relationships with students is as foundational to their daily practice as a stethoscope is to a physician. According to Dr. James P. Comer, a Yale professor and one of the world's leading child psychiatrists, "No significant learning can occur without a significant relationship" (Comer, 1995).

While you already understand the importance of relationships as a classroom leader, this chapter aims to enhance these skills by helping you uncover new insights as you continue to develop strong relationships with students, colleagues, parents, and community members. To achieve this requires analyzing both your relationships with others as well as with yourself.

Accordingly, you will be asked to reflect on guiding questions designed to reveal hidden thoughts or biases, enabling you to better serve and support others so they feel valued, seen, and heard. To start, it's important to understand that when leading other people, liking them is optional, but loving them is required.

Like vs. Love

Do you always like and enjoy every one of your students every day you teach them? Are there days when a student might do or say something that upsets you, forcing you to hopefully say the *second thing* that comes to your mind? Likewise, are there days when you might be a little less stressed or perhaps even relieved to learn that a certain student is going to be absent?

Regardless of whether you are a future or experienced teacher, you might be somewhat hesitant to respond. Admitting that you don't always like all your students could seem callous;

sometimes, the kids that can be a bit challenging are the ones who need their teachers the most. Let me ask another question: Do you love and care for every one of your students every minute they are in (and probably outside of) your class?

As we will learn in another chapter about the relational realities of leading others, "Two things can be true at once." As a teacher, it's entirely possible, and most likely probable, that while you love and care for all of your students, depending on the day or the individual, you might not always like them. Actually, it's not them personally; it's their choices and behavior, which is an important distinction for all leaders to make.

For those who might be wondering how teachers can still love a student on days when they don't particularly like their conduct, it's important to realize that "love" can be defined as kinship, affection, attachment, admiration, common interests, devotion, enthusiasm, loyal concern and value ("Love Definition & Meaning" (n.d.). Notice how the majority of words and phrases that define love reflect platonic relationships that can be expressed through appropriate words and behaviors.

For example, you can value your students and be concerned about them on days when you might not appreciate or like their behavior. Additionally, you can share common interests, be dedicated to and enthusiastic about a cause, and, at the same time, be upset or disappointed with your students' negative attitude or poor performance. However, even on the days when you might have reached your limit and become upset, you still love and care for your students.

Think about the favorite teacher you selected in Chapter 6. How did you feel when you upset or disappointed them? I imagine you felt pretty lousy because you respected them, and it was precisely because they loved and cared for you that you didn't want to disappoint them. Moreover, due to the relationship they had built with you and other students, you were more likely to go the extra mile in their class, even if it wasn't your favorite subject.

Accordingly, as a classroom teacher, you understand the importance of developing and sustaining relationships with your students. Because of this, I'm sure you would also agree that it's possible to temporarily dislike or be upset with someone yet still love them. Think about your own family members, friends, relatives, significant others, and so on. Are there days when you are upset or annoyed with them and, in the moment, don't particularly like them? Absolutely. Does this mean you no longer care for or love them? Of course not! Two things can be true at once.

As a full-time, professional people influencer, you are keenly aware that human beings – regardless of their age, height, grade level, or professional accomplishments – will not fully invest in another person (such as their teacher or boss) until they know that person has their best interest at heart. As the old adage goes, "People don't care how much you know until they know how much you care."

To lead is to build relationships, and authentic, meaningful relationships can only be built upon a loving foundation. Because of this, teachers understand one of the great paradoxes of leadership: We can and must love, care for, support, and serve others even when and if we don't like them.

In their best-selling book *What Happened to You?: Conversations on Trauma, Resilience, and Healing* (which I encourage every educator to read), Dr. Bruce Perry and Oprah Winfrey (2021) remind us that "the most powerful form of reward is relational. Positive interactions with people are rewarding and regulating" (p. 66). Classroom teachers understand that we must first develop healthy relationships with those we serve before we can positively and consistently influence them. I feel so strongly about the power of relationships and leading with love that it's part of my personal leadership definition and included in the Teacher-Leader's Credo: "Relationships and influence are not optional."

However, when I work with current and aspiring leaders outside of PreK-12, next to addressing conflict, the notion of developing relationships with others and *ahem, loving them*, especially if they don't like them, can be odd, uncomfortable, and difficult to comprehend. Nevertheless, as Clay Scroggins (2017) says in his book *How to Lead When You're Not in Charge*, "Loving someone and leading them are a package deal. You can't have one without the other" (p. 192). Simply stated, You gotta love 'em to lead 'em.

As a great leader, you recognize the importance of showing up each day to serve your students and lead with love. You understand this is foundational to creating a space in which they feel safe and motivated to try, make mistakes, and ultimately learn and grow. In fact, the relationship you establish with a kid might be one of the few safe and nurturing relationships in their life. Because of this, more so than almost any other profession, you understand while liking those we serve is optional, loving them is non-negotiable. The following acronym – especially on difficult days – can be a powerful reminder to always lead with love, regardless of whom we are serving:

Lead

Others with

Vulnerability and

Empathy

Your Relationship With Others

As a classroom teacher, I know you not only develop healthy relationships with your students but also understand the distinction between liking and loving them. However, my experience working with teacher leaders suggests that developing relationships with adults such as colleagues, parents, and stakeholders can be more challenging and may cause some anxiety. Teachers may be less likely to pursue leadership roles outside of their classrooms because of their fear or hesitancy to lead other adults, especially those they don't get along with or care for.

However, I have some comforting news: It's not just you, and it's certainly not because you're a teacher. It's because you and the adults you would lead are all human. A simple search on Google or Amazon will reveal many resources specifically designed to help leaders in every profession and industry better understand those they serve and build healthy working relationships. Similar to Dr. Comer's quote at the beginning of this chapter, it's difficult for anything of value or substance to occur within *any* organization in the absence of significant relationships.

Therefore, the following questions are designed to help you reflect upon how you develop relationships with others based on your interactions, preferred communication styles, and relationship patterns. When possible, try to think about the different people with whom you have a relationship, such as your students, colleagues or family members. Please note that this activity will take some time and require deep reflection, honesty, and vulnerability.

Interaction with Others
- How do you typically interact with others?
- Are you a good listener?
- Do you maintain eye contact during conversations?
- Do you find yourself interrupting others when they speak?
- How do others perceive you? Ask a trusted friend or colleague familiar with your communication style if you have unintentional behaviors that could be perceived as rude, unprofessional, or aloof.

Preferred Communication
- What is your preferred mode of communicating with others?
- How do you prefer your leaders to communicate with you?
- Think of positive and negative relationships you have had and try to identify how styles and modes of communication affected the relationship.

Relationship Patterns
- Do your relationships generally follow a positive or negative pattern?
- How do these patterns affect your approach to professional relationships?
- Are you aware of any recurring relationship dynamics that might influence your professional interactions?

Building Relationships
- How do you typically go about building relationships with others?
- Is it easier for you to build relationships in personal or professional settings?

- What strategies do you use to form connections with others?
- Do you find building relationships to be generally easy or difficult?

Now that you have hopefully answered and reflected upon these questions, review them and, where applicable, ask yourself the following:

- Is there a significant difference in how you would respond or behave to certain questions if they referred to a student instead of another adult?
- Why are there differences?
- How can you effectively apply your student-based leadership and relationship-building skills to adults? What aspects would be similar, and what areas would be different?

Your Relationship With Yourself

If you recall from a previous chapter, even though leaders spend most of their time influencing others, the first person we must lead each day is ourselves. Remember, "It's not about me, but it starts with me." Great leaders know who they are, what they do, why they do it, and for whom they do it. In addition, they establish and maintain acceptable, healthy boundaries in which this occurs. In other words, they have a healthy relationship with themselves, which affects how they interact and develop relationships with others.

Imagine it's a typical school day, and you are at home going through your morning routine and about to leave the house. What is the one item you must have, or you will go back home and get before arriving at school?

Please know there's zero judgment here! For some, it might be your phone, laptop or tablet. For others, it might be your lunch because you like to prepare meals that can be consumed quickly while walking, talking, grading a paper, supervising students, and making a few copies. Additionally, you may have said your morning coffee or go-to drink, without which teaching is almost impossible, especially on Mondays!

There's one more item that people often fail to mention, but it's actually the most important. In fact, it's the one thing that is universal. Everyone must take this to work every day of their career: themselves. That's right. The one thing that we *always* bring to work is ourselves and everything that comes with us.

This is important because *who* we bring to school each day and our relationship with that person will affect our thoughts, behaviors, and subsequent interactions with everyone else. Just like parents send the best and only version of their child to school each day (trust me, they're not leaving a different version at home just to keep you on your toes), you, too, are the only person who can leave your house to show up to teach your students.

In addition to showing up for your students, the best teacher in your house is also the only one who can show up to work with and support your colleagues. As Dr. Perry (2021) says in *What Happened to You?* "The sense of self informs every relationship or decision we make as we move through life" (p. 36). Our relationship with ourselves – how we think about and treat ourselves – directly affects our relationships with others.

To better identify potential blind spots you may have that could unknowingly impede your ability to effectively lead others, especially adults, answer the following sets of questions, preferably taking the time to write out your responses. Similar to developing your mission statement, focus on the key actions, characteristics, and traits. Please note that this activity is not intended to trigger you or cause negative emotions, so only respond to the questions in a manner in which you are comfortable.

In The Past

Think about a time in the past, perhaps middle or high school, and answer the following questions:

1. What type of student were you in school? How did you behave? From your current perspective as a teacher, how would you describe yourself if you were one of your students?
2. Describe the type of friends, classmates, or peers you enjoyed being around and why.
3. Describe the type of friends, classmates, or peers you did not enjoy being around or those who perhaps upset you and why.
4. If you ever made a poor choice and got in trouble, what happened, and to what extent did it involve other people and some type of relationship? Did this continue, and if so, what were some of the patterns?

In The Present

Now think about your more recent experiences, which include your adult and professional life, and respond to the following:

5. Describe the type of person you prefer to work with. Why do you prefer and feel comfortable around this type of person?
6. Describe the type of person you prefer not to work with or perhaps dislike. Why do you prefer not to work with and/or dislike and feel uncomfortable around this type of person?

7. What are some of the primary behaviors or characteristics in another person that bring you joy, causing you to feel at ease?
8. What are some of the primary behaviors or characteristics in another person that irritate you, causing you to feel anxious?
9. Describe the type of person you are typically close to or with whom you typically develop a positive friendship or relationship.
10. Describe the type of person with whom you may have had a previous friendship and/or relationship, but there was some falling out.
11. Describe the type of person with whom you typically don't develop a positive friendship or relationship.

Common Themes

The questions you just responded to were designed to help you better identify past and current habits and experiences with relationships and how that might help or hinder your ability to develop healthy, professional relationships with those you serve, especially when leading adults. These questions focused on the following themes, each of which will be further discussed to identify strengths, weaknesses, potential biases, and areas for growth.

- Personality Preferences
- Behavioral Traits
- Relational and Social Dynamics
- Conflict and Challenges

Personality Preferences

Consisting of questions 2, 5, and 6, this theme focuses on the types of people or overall personality traits and character with whom you prefer to associate, along with those you might dislike or prefer not to work with. Looking at your responses to these questions, how have these preferences changed or remained the same from the past to the present, especially within your professional life? Are there personality traits you once disliked but now value, or vice versa?

It's important to consider these preferences, how they were formed, and if they have changed over time, especially those that might be negative. For example, the type of personality traits you listed as not preferring to be around or work with are just that – a set of traits and not necessarily an actual human being. Nonetheless, when confronted with these traits, especially when leading adults, we naturally resort to our feelings and past experiences and unknowingly favor or exclude someone because they remind us of someone else.

Accordingly, identify a few of these overarching personality preferences and be mindful of them, realizing that not every person who may present those traits is exactly like the person or those who initially formed your past feelings. Whether they're a student, colleague, or parent, your job is to lead with love and treat them fairly.

Behavioral Traits

Questions 1, 7, and 8 focused on specific behavioral traits or actions people display that dictate whether or not you prefer to associate or work with them. Thinking about your own behavioral traits, especially around others, what has remained the same over the years, and what has changed? To what extent has this been affected by your professional training and subsequent experience? Are there areas you have identified that would be helpful to address regarding your ability to build relationships with and lead others effectively?

Similar to your personality preferences, it's important to acknowledge some specific behaviors you are either drawn to or dislike and be cognizant that it may affect how you treat others and ultimately form relationships with them. For example, identify two to three behaviors that tend to upset you, especially if they have been persistent since you were younger. Have you ever unknowingly shown bias towards others who displayed these traits? How can you intentionally work to address this in the future?

Relational and Social Dynamics

As you may now realize, how we form relationships with others and ourselves is symbiotic. What's more, while differences and boundaries exist between our personal and professional relationships, the foundation of who we are and how we relate to others affects all areas of our lives. Figure 8.1 illustrates the similarities and differences between our relationships with ourselves and others and acknowledges the intersection of the two within our personal and professional lives. From a relationship standpoint, this represents the person we bring to work each day.

Figure 8.1: Spheres of Relationships

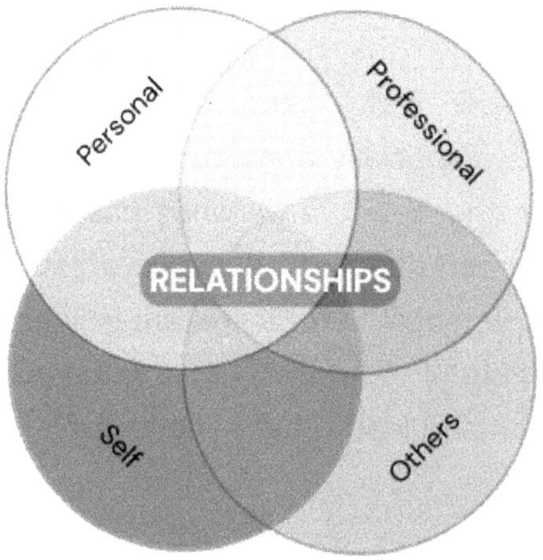

Questions 2, 3, 9, and 11 can provide insight into the dynamics of your relationships, personally and professionally. In addition to asking about the type of people with whom you typically develop friendships, a few of these questions were also designed to uncover the type of people with whom you don't prefer to associate or by whom you may have unfortunately been treated poorly, including being the victim of bullying.

As you reflect upon your responses to these questions, consider how your professional or work friends might differ from your personal friends. Questions 2 and 3 focus on the past; 9 and 11 discuss the present. To what extent have you changed, or perhaps grown, in these areas, and how have you stayed the same? What have you learned about yourself in terms of being able to maintain healthy relationships?

Finally, looking at the pattern of your responses, including what has remained the same over the years, what type of social dynamics, groups, or teams do you prefer to be a part of? Another way to think about this is to consider what "lunch table" you currently prefer to sit at (or are invited to), especially as a professional.

Conversely, what social dynamics and groups do you either not wish to be a part of or, for various reasons, might cause you to feel angry, anxious, or fearful? In other words, what lunch table do you either not want to sit at or, perhaps, are upset that you were never invited?

While it's important to identify your blind spots and areas of unintentional bias that might hinder how you develop relationships with others and subsequently lead them, this theme is especially important because it's very personal. Therefore, within a professional context, are there people, probably other adults, about whom you have made unfair assumptions (positively or negatively), thus including or excluding them from your professional circle or lunch table?

Based on your past experiences and current preferences, have you inadvertently formed cliques that send the message that some are favored while others are excluded? If so, don't worry; you're human, and simply being aware of this can now enable you to be more intentional about how you interact with others based upon feelings and assumptions that might not be valid.

Remember, just because your colleague or a student's parent reminds you of someone who upset you in the past, it's a completely different person, and just like you do with your own students, you must separate the behavior from the individual, be professional, and address what's in front of you.

Conflict and Challenges

It's important to realize that how we approach conflict, and the associated challenges is related to how we get along with ourselves and others. Questions 4 and 10 are related to this theme, one of which asks about whether or not you made poor choices in the past, and the other focuses on a more current relationship that might have ended poorly. It's important to recognize how we have made choices that have led to negative consequences within the context of leading others. Remember, of all the choices you have and will make in your life, be it positive or negative, the one consistent factor is you. Regardless of who else might have been involved, you were there for all of it.

As you review your responses to these two questions, to what extent has your approach to addressing relational-based conflict and challenges changed? What have you learned, and how have you grown? In addition, is there a pattern or connection between your personal and professional relationships? What's one area you would like to work on?

As you know, some form of conflict occurs daily in every leader's life, and while you might be fairly comfortable addressing conflict among your students, it can be more difficult with other adults. Accordingly, what biases might have emerged from this theme's questions? Are there certain assumptions you might be more likely to make about some people, thus causing you to assume they're more prone to being wrong, making bad choices, or causing conflict and challenges? As a leader, how can you better recognize this in the future to more effectively and professionally serve others while also addressing problems?

Table 8.1 visually represents the questions and related themes you just answered and analyzed. In addition, this table includes an additional column, Potential Bias & Future Actions. Take some time to review your responses to the questions along with the additional answers and realizations that may have emerged after reading the four themes. Based on these themes and questions, try to identify a bias – albeit unintentional – you may have that could negatively impact how you develop relationships with others, especially those whom you might be asked to lead in a professional setting.

For each row, write down any potential biases that may have emerged and try to identify past and present reasons that may have contributed to this bias and how you can address it in the future. Remember, leadership is a day job; developing and sustaining relationships is an intentional, daily habit.

Table 8.1: Relationship Themes, Questions, Biases, and Actions

Themes	Past Questions	Present Questions	Potential Bias & Future Actions
Personality Preferences	Describe the type of friends, classmates, or peers you enjoyed being around and why.	Describe the type of person you prefer to work with. Why do you prefer and feel comfortable around this type of person? Describe the type of person you prefer not to work with or perhaps dislike. Why do you prefer not to work with and/or dislike and feel uncomfortable around this type of person?	
Behavioral Traits	What type of student were you in school? How did you behave? From your current perspective as a teacher, how would you describe yourself if you were one of your students?	What are some of the primary behaviors or characteristics in another person that bring you joy, causing you to feel at ease? What are some of the primary behaviors or characteristics in another person that irritate you, causing you to feel anxious?	

Themes	Past Questions	Present Questions	Potential Bias & Future Actions
Relational and Social Dynamics	Describe the type of friends, classmates, or peers you enjoyed being around and why. Describe the type of friends, classmates, or peers you did not enjoy being around or those who perhaps upset you and why.	Describe the type of person you are typically close to and/or with whom you typically develop a positive friendship and/or relationship. Describe the type of person with whom you typically don't develop a positive friendship and/or relationship.	
Conflict and Challenges	If you ever made a poor choice and got in trouble, what happened, and to what extent did it involve other people and some type of relationship? Did this continue, and if so, what were some of the patterns?	Describe the person with whom you may have had a positive friendship or relationship, but there was some falling out.	

Whether it's a teacher in a classroom or the president of a large corporation, leaders must first develop healthy, professional relationships with everyone they serve to influence others positively. This requires leaders to be vulnerable and acknowledge that despite their backgrounds, experiences, and personal preferences, they must choose daily to serve others with love, especially those with whom they have little in common or may not particularly like. As a classroom teacher, you are uniquely prepared and qualified to build positive, unbiased relationships with everyone you serve inside and outside your classroom.

Discussion and Application Questions

1. What did you learn about yourself, and how do you build relationships with others that you can immediately apply as they relate to students, colleagues, or stakeholders?
2. In reviewing the themes and related past and present questions, what was one significant takeaway or aha moment you realized about how you may unknowingly show bias to others? What will you do to address this?
3. To what extent do you feel more comfortable or empowered to develop healthy, professional relationships with adults while serving as their leader?

References

Comer, J. P. (1995). *Untitled lecture.* Lecture presented at the Education Service Center, Region IV, Houston, TX.

"Love Definition & Meaning." (n.d.). *Merriam-Webster.* https://www.merriam-webster.com/dictionary/love

Perry, B. D., & Winfrey, O. (2021). *What happened to you?: Conversations on trauma, resilience, and healing.* [Kindle version]. Flatiron. https://a.co/d/9Hwwhm8

Scroggins, C. (2017). *How to lead when you're not in charge: Leveraging influence when you lack authority.* [Kindle version]. Zondervan. https://a.co/d/0IZUsuP

CHAPTER 9

Culture and Climate: We All Live Here

"We all have the opportunity and ability to create our own culture."
~Dr. David Arencibia

When asked to define "culture," some people may reference a physical place or country with its people, food, language, and customs. They may think about what people do and how they behave. Similarly, when asked to define "climate," some might mention the weather or environment of a specific region, indicating if it's hot, dry, or cold. Both of these definitions are accurate and somewhat interrelated; a country's culture can be influenced and affected by its climate and vice versa.

Organizations also have their respective culture and climate, and just like other countries, these two elements are interrelated and will always occur and be present in some form. The moment we step into a culture and its climate, such as a classroom, school, or district office, two things happen regardless of our intentionality or actions:

1. We are affected by the culture and climate and those within it.
2. We affect the culture and climate and those within it.

An organization's culture and climate are much like a swimming pool; everyone's in it together, and there's no such thing as a clean and unclean section. A small drop of something toxic or undesirable can ruin the water for everyone. In fact, a Glassdoor (2019) survey of over 5,000 respondents confirms the significance of organizational culture, finding that 77% of adults would consider a company's culture before applying for a job there, with over 50% indicating that a company's culture is more important to them than the salary ("Culture Over Cash?", 2019).

Indeed, an organization's culture and climate are not only everything but everywhere, representing the environment in which people live and carry out their professional lives. While culture and climate are everyone's responsibility, they start with and are a direct reflection of the organization's formal leaders.

Before moving on, it's important to note that the word culture is often used in a way that also encompasses climate, both of which will be explored in this chapter. If you have studied or read about organizational culture, you may have encountered the term used as an overarching concept that includes aspects of climate, which is perfectly acceptable. However, while it might seem like splitting hairs, I believe there is value in distinguishing between culture and climate when training leaders, especially those working in educational organizations.

Defining Culture and Climate

According to Merriam-Webster, culture is defined as "the set of shared attitudes, values, goals, and practices that characterizes an institution or organization" ("Culture Definition & Meaning," n.d.). More specific to leadership, John Maxwell (2020) defines a company's culture as "the expression of the values of the people within the organization" (p. 27).

John Amaechi defines culture as "The worst behavior tolerated" (Grant, 2021). I am particularly fond of this definition since it resonates with classroom teachers and applies to any organization's culture, serving as a reminder that leaders encourage what they tolerate and normalize what they ignore.

Big "C" and Little "c" Culture

As an educator, my background is in bilingual and foreign language education, having taught English as a Second Language (ESL) and Spanish as a classroom teacher. I mention this because those familiar with this field are probably aware of the terms Big "C" and Little "c" culture, which I find relevant to distinguishing between organizational culture and climate.

Big C culture refers to a country, group, or organization's products, values, beliefs, and behaviors. Aligning with the traditional definition of culture, Big C is more generalized and reflects how most people, whether unfamiliar with or not native to that culture, would describe it. In other words, Big C culture reflects a country's known traditions; it's *what people do* and *how they do it* (Herron et al., 2013).

Whereas Big C culture can be viewed from a distance, Little c requires a more in-depth understanding of the actual daily practices within that culture. This reflects a more intimate and foundational understanding, thus revealing the *why* behind people's values, beliefs, and behaviors and *how it feels* to be immersed and live in that culture. In my opinion, Little c culture refers to the *climate* that exists within a given culture.

Think about the type of culture in most PreK-12 schools in the United States. While there are certainly variations, the reason that teachers receive a license to teach a certain grade level or subject and not for a specific school building or district is because the culture of PreK-12 education is similar enough that most properly credentialed teachers can easily adapt and integrate into almost any school in the country.

For example, the what and how of PreK-12 public education (the culture) are more similar than different due to state and federal rules and regulations. Many common traditions are known and visible to those familiar with schools, similar to what we might know about countries we have never visited.

However, just as it's necessary to visit a country and spend time doing what the locals do daily to understand their climate better, the same is true within organizations. To understand climate – which is related to but different from the culture – one must be immersed in the organization to know why things are done and, more importantly, how it feels to live there and experience it.

Understanding Culture and Climate

Creating and sustaining an effective culture and climate is a fundamental responsibility for leaders everywhere. An organization's culture and climate set the tone and comfort level for those who work and live in it, along with sending a message to external stakeholders.

Therefore, intentionally creating and sustaining a healthy organizational culture and climate is a characteristic and trait of all great leaders and a non-negotiable, pre-requisite skill for classroom teachers. However, the unfortunate truth is that some leaders in other industries can get by or survive (i.e., keep their jobs) despite their inability to create a positive culture and climate.

This is partly because some leaders are neither literally nor figuratively standing at the head of the organization, in front of everyone they serve, on a daily, minute-by-minute basis. In some instances, those on the ground floor of the organization may never see or interact with their leaders. Sadly, some leaders can eschew their responsibility to create a healthy organizational culture and climate by choosing to hide out, thus minimizing their visibility.

However, as tempting as it might be some days, classroom teachers can't just hide out and choose to be invisible to their students. Once again, teachers are the epitome of yet another great leadership trait in that they *must create and sustain a positive classroom culture and climate for those they serve on a daily basis.* Additionally, teachers are responsible for leading multiple micro-cultures and climates within the same day since each class or group of students is unique, thus representing its own traditions (cultures), rationale, and feelings (climate).

Not including the building and district in which you currently work, think about some of the best cultures (and associated climates) that you have been a part of, such as groups, teams, organizations, or places you have worked, and answer the following questions:

- What were some shared attitudes, values, goals, and expectations? What did this culture do?
- How did people express these attitudes, values, goals, and expectations? Why did this culture do it?
- What was encouraged, tolerated, allowed, and/or ignored, and how did this contribute to the overall culture and climate?
- How did it *feel* to work in this culture's *climate*? How would you describe the climate?
- How did you feel on Sundays when thinking about entering this culture and climate on Monday?
- To what extent were external stakeholders drawn to or away from this culture and climate?

Take some time to specifically reflect upon the culture and climate in the following areas of your current professional life (classroom, school, and district), identifying *the what*, *the how*, and *the traditions* (culture), along with *why* things are done and *how it feels* to be part of that environment (climate).

Your Classroom

Remember, you are the CEO of your classroom, and while you certainly have to work in the overall environment prevalent in your school and district, within the four walls of your room, you are the leader; you set the tone, cast the vision, and establish and promote your desired culture and climate.

Reflecting upon your own classroom, answer the following questions:

- How would you describe your classroom culture?
- How would you describe your classroom climate?
- What are the values, goals, behaviors, and practices you promote and reinforce daily within your classroom?
- What do you encourage, tolerate, allow, and ignore?
- Do your students know why you are passionate about what you do?
- Do your students understand why caring and contributing in your classroom is important?
- How do you want students to feel in your classroom?
- What do you want your students to experience in your classroom?
- How do you feel on Sundays about the specific thought of going into your classroom (not the school or district) on Monday?

Review your answers and identify at least one area in which you can intentionally focus to improve or enhance an aspect of your classroom culture and climate. What will this further enable your students to do, become, feel, and/or experience?

Your School and District

Moving outside of your classroom, how would you describe the culture and climate of your school building and district? While all teachers are leaders and CEOs of their respective classrooms, this is where the impact and effectiveness of your upper-level administrative team is critically important. This is where, for better or worse, their leadership acumen is on display and cascades from the top down, affecting students, staffulty, and stakeholders.

Accordingly, while we certainly need to keep great teachers in the classroom, we also need to ensure that those who do leave to lead are doing so for the right reasons and are adequately prepared.

Since leadership is leadership, everything presented thus far in this book is as relevant to you as a teacher leader as it is to your building and district-level administrators or any other leader in your community. In addition, if you have read to this point, you can no longer claim ignorance when it comes to recognizing and knowing how to build upon your natural leadership skills to influence and support others, which includes your building and district administrators.

When principals and superintendents talk about the need to build leadership capacity within their teams, it includes developing leaders who are good teammates. These teacher leaders should be as effective as they are compassionate and understanding, helping carry out the administrative vision and thus supporting the culture and climate of the organization.

Because of this, before addressing the culture and climate questions related to your school and district, please consider the following from the Teacher-Leader's Credo: just like you, your leaders are only human, and they appreciate and deserve some grace along with the benefit of the doubt.

- Your leaders will never be perfect, but neither will those they serve (this includes you).
- Your leaders are in the people business, and people are messy; both you and your administrators are messy people.

- Sometimes, your irresponsibility becomes your leaders' responsibility. They address it because they realize it's not about them, but it starts with them.
- Just because leaders are vulnerable and acknowledge that people see their faults, whether they admit them or not, does not necessarily mean they want others to point it out and rub their noses in it.
- Conflict happens every day in the life of a leader. Addressing it while maintaining strong relationships with those you serve involves acknowledging that good people can make bad choices. For a building administrator, that group of good people includes not only students but also you and your colleagues.

Finally, although it's not specifically reflected in the Credo, remember that your leaders earn their money on the hard days, addressing conflict and making difficult decisions that very few people see, appreciate, or understand, often choosing between bad or worse. (I can assure you they would choose between good or great for free!)

Showing them grace means stepping back and assuming positive intent before your default response to unmet expectations or dismissing the physical and emotional toll the job takes on them and their families is, "That's why they get paid the big bucks!" Anyone who has ever looked at what their leaders do and thought, "You couldn't pay me enough to do that," has essentially acknowledged their leader's worth.

Therefore, from a perspective in which you are not only a teammate but also an effective, compassionate, and capable leader, please reflect upon the following questions, thinking about how you can serve, support, and be part of the solution when it comes to the overall culture and climate within your school and district. (If you are preparing to be a teacher, you can answer these based on schools and districts you've been in; you could interview a current teacher or answer in a way that reflects the type of culture and climate you hope to be a part of.)

- How would you describe the culture of your school and district?
- How would you describe the climate of your school and district?
- To what extent can staff/ty in your school and district explain your administration's vision? For example, is there some form of branding like a logo, saying, or acronym everyone knows and applies?
- To what extent are there differences in the culture and climate within your school and that of the district?
- At both the building and district level, what's encouraged, tolerated, allowed, and ignored? How does this (positively or negatively) affect the culture and climate?
- If you're in a district with multiple attendance centers, are there marked differences in the culture and climate within those buildings, and to what extent does it reflect or align with that of the district?
- What are the values, goals, behaviors, and practices your school and district leaders promote and reinforce daily?
- How does it feel to live and work in your building and district on a daily basis?
- How would you describe your stakeholders' (parents and community members) relationship with and support of your school and district?
- How do you feel on Sunday at the thought of starting another week in your building and district?

- Would you recommend working in this school and district to a qualified friend or family member? Why or why not?

While I'm hopeful that everyone reading these questions could say they are currently working in a great culture and climate, it doesn't take a math teacher to know this is statistically impossible. (People wouldn't read books like this and ask me to come speak and train their leaders if every place was perfect!) Therefore, it's likely that some of you have either worked in or are currently in an environment where the culture and climate that your formal leadership *allows* (that's right, it starts with them) is somewhere on the spectrum from "We could get better" to "We wish we could leave!"

While you are in charge of your classroom and everything that occurs within those four walls, it's also possible that you and some of your colleagues are like an oasis in the desert, serving as an anomaly to the prevalent culture and climate, offering a welcome reprieve to those who enter. However, it is nonetheless my hope that in realizing your inherent leadership abilities, you feel empowered to continue to support your leaders while also serving your students and community. I encourage you to work to be part of the solution instead of unknowingly contributing to the problem.

At the same time, however, please note that while it is outside the scope of this book to provide expert advice on if and when someone should leave the classroom or profession altogether, if you are in a situation where you are being treated poorly or in a manner that violates your rights, please seek help from those who can advocate for and support you.

Four Pillars of Leading An Effective Culture and Climate

Remaining consistent with my goal of helping you develop as a leader, I would like to share my Four Pillars of Leading An

Effective Culture and Climate. Please understand that while this is certainly relevant to all areas of leadership, including your own classroom, it will also add value to you in the event you are asked to transition into formalized teacher leader roles working with your colleagues and other adults, which we know can be challenging.

1. Culture and climate are a full-time responsibility.
2. Culture and climate are a shared responsibility.
3. Culture and climate are created each day.
4. Culture and climate require change.

As you work through these four pillars, revisit the mission statement you developed in Chapter 6, and use it as a guide, ensuring alignment with your mission and how you react to the four pillars. Also, review the Daily H.A.B.I.T.S. and the Leader's Daily Five from Chapter 7 (See Table 9.1), and try to identify how each of these could also guide or inform how you would go about promoting an effective culture and climate.

Culture and Climate Is a Full-Time Responsibility
At the start of this chapter, I mentioned that culture and climate are everywhere and everything, and each time we step into an environment, the following occurs:

- We are affected by the culture and climate and those within it.
- We affect the culture and climate and those within it.

You may also recall from Chapter 7 that Leadership is a Day Job, which means leaders are always on. Therefore, as a teacher, you are a full-time, walking, talking, billboard for who you are as a leader, which is a direct reflection of the culture and climate you create for those you serve. Consequently, on a daily basis, your conduct, words, habits, decisions, and treatment of others must be *intentional* and in line with your desired culture and climate.

I suspect that you understand this because whenever a student sees you in the real world, such as the grocery store, without thinking, you go into teacher mode and intentionally treat them and their family as if they were in your classroom, thus reflecting your culture and climate. This is not because you are being disingenuous or putting on a show; it's your character; it's who you are because you know what you do, why you do it, whom you serve, and how you want them to feel.

Accordingly, look at your mission statement and ask what that looks like daily, both inside and outside your classroom. How must you talk to and about others to align with your mission? How must you treat others?

Finally, think about a scenario outside of your classroom that may involve influencing adults. How might you be able to intentionally promote and reflect your culture and climate when working with them? For example, if the socially acceptable thing to do in your classroom is to treat others with kindness, then ensure you are modeling that in your behavior towards others.

Overall, developing and supporting the culture and climate that reflects who you are as a leader and subsequently affects the actions, behaviors, and feelings of those you serve is a full-time, daily responsibility.

Culture and Climate Is a Shared Responsibility

While you are responsible for promoting and affecting your culture and climate, it is also a shared responsibility. For some leaders, this can be one of the more difficult and frustrating pillars. Although it's important to *articulate* your desired culture and climate, it can be more challenging to *actuate* it, which requires positively influencing other people's behavior daily.

For example, if you're an experienced teacher, think back to your very first day in the classroom as a *real teacher*. Although I'm confident you had some ability when it came to establishing and managing the expectations and behavior in your room (i.e., the culture and climate), it's one thing to write it down as part of a college assignment or even present it to your students' parents during back to school night; it's completely different when the rubber meets the road, and you must actually get a bunch of little humans to comply – and then repeat it 179 more times until the end of the year!

In fact, I'm positive that many of you take the time to establish and agree upon classroom norms and expectations with your students at the start of the school year. Granted, as the teacher, you know your non-negotiables, but as an effective leader, you start by casting the vision and, within those parameters, empower those you serve – your students – by asking for input, thus sharing the responsibility for promoting the culture and climate within your classroom.

Focusing outside of your classroom, think about a time when you and your colleagues collaborated to accomplish something, and it was either a negative experience or the end result failed to meet expectations. To what extent would it have been helpful if you and others had been empowered and given a sense of shared responsibility to not only affect the final outcome but, more importantly, the culture and climate within the group?

Finally, think about the culture and climate within your current school, building, or district. What steps can you take each day to intentionally contribute to the organizational culture and climate by sharing some form of responsibility?

Culture and Climate Are Created Each Day

Over forty years ago, business management experts Tom Peters and Robert Waterman (1982) published *In Search of Excellence: Lessons from America's Best-Run Companies*. This innovative approach to leadership introduced the concept of "Management by Walking Around" (MBWA), which encouraged managers to leave their offices, be visible, interact with their teams, and develop relationships with those they served.

However, nearly four decades after the introduction of MBWA, a 2016 survey by Harris Poll found that 69% (of more than 2,000 managers surveyed) still felt uncomfortable communicating with their employees. Additionally, 37% reported discomfort in giving direct feedback about performance, fearing negative reactions (Solomon, 2016).

As a classroom teacher, you not only understand the importance of walking around and interacting with your students and building relationships with them *every day* (do you ever get to sit down?), but anytime you address a wrong answer or give a less-than-perfect grade on an assignment, you're also providing feedback that may cause someone to react negatively. This is yet another example of how PreK-12 teachers are excellent, natural leaders and have a deep understanding of how to develop and sustain a positive culture and climate with their students.

I especially like what Dr. Joe Sanfelippo, a well-known author, speaker, and district superintendent, says about culture: "Culture is built in 30-second increments. Every time you connect with someone in your school or community, you are building or killing culture" (X, n.d.).

Whether your intentions are positive, negative, or non-existent, everything you do and say, each interaction with every person, is essentially taking a step towards or away from building your desired culture and climate and reflecting your character as a leader.

Culture and climate are created each day based on leaders' intentional habits, which involve interacting with and influencing others. Similar to how most of us with a PreK-12 background are familiar with the phrase "Every kid. Every day," as leaders, we must take that same approach with our colleagues and stakeholders: "Every interaction. Every day."

This concept is especially important to realize when interacting with those with whom you might have little in common or simply dislike; they might need the reinforcement of a positive culture and climate the most. In *Atomic Habits*, James Clear (2018) states that "Every action you take is a vote for the person you wish to become" (p. 35). Likewise, as a leader, every action you take is also a vote for the type of culture and climate in which you and those you serve will live.

Therefore, I encourage you to be intentional about every interaction you have – especially those outside of your classroom in support of colleagues, administration, and stakeholders – and realize you have the opportunity, 30 seconds at a time, to positively affect and add value to others in a way that is consistent with your culture, climate, and overall character.

Figure 9.1: 4 Pillars of Leading an Effective Culture and Climate

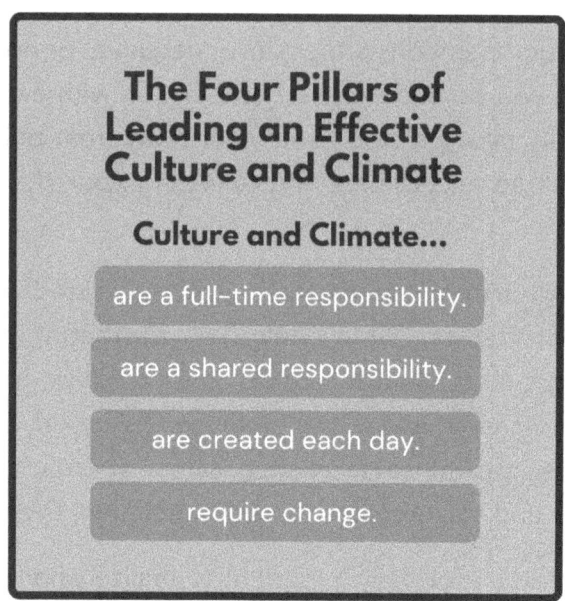

Culture and Climate Requires Change

In Heather Forbes' book, *Help for Billy: A Beyond Consequences Approach to Helping Children in the Classroom* (which is a great resource for helping kids with complex trauma), she shares a quote by King Whitney, Jr., that effectively captures how most people, regardless of their age or circumstances, view change:

> Change has a considerable psychological impact on the human mind. To the fearful it is threatening because it means that things may get worse. To the hopeful it is encouraging because things may get better. To the confident it is inspiring because the challenge exists to make things better. (As cited in Forbes, 2013, p. 105)

To what extent does this resonate with you? Have there been times in your professional life in which a potential change has led you and others to believe things might get worse? Have you ever been encouraged that a possible change could offer an improvement, or perhaps felt empowered to take an active role to personally make things better?

Similar to how we all affect and are affected by culture and climate, regardless of our intentions, the same can be said about change. Regardless of what we do, want, or wish for, change always occurs; progress is perpetual.

For example, no two days are the same. As you read this now, the day you are in will never again exist. Even though you might teach the same lessons or content for many years, no two classes or school years are the same.

If you recall from the Teacher-Leader's Credo, "I must give up to go up. What got me here won't get me there." This emphasizes the fact that from an organizational standpoint, culture and climate are fluid—they keep moving and changing regardless of whether we are active or apathetic, contribute or complain.

While leaders must be intentional about maintaining some level of consistency within their respective culture and climate, at the same time, it takes courage and vulnerability to recognize that life goes on within every organization either *because of* or *in spite of* the leaders' intentions and actions. Change represents growth, which is never comfortable. As Brené Brown (2017) says, "We can choose courage, or we can choose comfort, but we can't have both. Not at the same time" (p. 4).

Consider the following questions related to possible changes you have experienced:

- What are some examples of changes you've experienced in your school or district?

- To what extent did these changes affect your daily classroom practice?
- Were all of your colleagues, stakeholders, and community members on board with these changes? Why or why not?
- To what extent did you support these changes? In retrospect, could you have been more positive and supportive?

While we may have little to no control over changes within our culture and climate, we have complete control over how we respond with our attitude, actions, and contributions. We are all allotted 24 hours a day, which means it takes just as long to be resistant and unproductive by complaining about something as it does to be productive and choose to be part of the solution. As a leader, choose to support those who support you, and be open and positive about the inherent changes that occur within the culture and climate of every organization.

Table 9.1 Integrating Culture & Climate, H.A.B.I.T.S. & Daily Five

Four Pillars of Leading An Effective Culture & Climate	Daily H.A.B.I.T.S.	Leader's Daily Five
Culture and climate are a full-time responsibility	Intentional Self-Care and Development	Would I want to be my leader today? Am I improving others by improving myself?
Culture and climate are a shared responsibility	Belief in Others Talk and Treat	Whom am I serving today? Who needs me today?
Culture and climate are created each day	Attitude and Affirmations Talk and Treat	Would I want to be my leader today? Am I willing to be uncomfortable for others?

Four Pillars of Leading An Effective Culture & Climate	Daily H.A.B.I.T.S.	Leader's Daily Five
Culture and climate require change.	Here and Now Self-Care and Development	Would I want to be my leader today? Am I improving others by improving myself?

Although culture and climate permeate everything we do and experience within our respective organizations, some leaders may find it challenging to fully embrace these concepts, particularly if they feel uncomfortable building relationships with those they serve. However, as a teacher, you are uniquely qualified and positioned to create and nurture a healthy culture and climate both inside and outside of your classroom. This happens each day, interaction by interaction, 30 seconds at a time. By doing so, you not only ensure that all your students feel safe and valued, which is crucial for their success but also contribute to a positive environment among your colleagues and stakeholders, supporting and enhancing the overall culture and climate of your school and district.

Discussion and Application Questions

1. Revisit Table 9.1 and your Mission Statement. To what extent is there alignment that supports the type of culture and climate you have or hope to create within your classroom?
2. Which of the Four Pillars of Leading an Effective Culture and Climate are you most comfortable with as a leader within your classroom, school and district?
3. Which of the Four Pillars of Leading an Effective Culture and Climate are you least comfortable with as a leader within your classroom, school and district?

4. What strategies have you found effective in embracing and supporting change in your classroom, school and district?
5. How do you balance the need for consistency with the necessity of change?

References

Brown, B. (2017). *Rising strong: How the ability to reset transforms the way we live, love, parent, and lead.* Random House.

Clear, J. (2018). *Atomic habits: Tiny changes, remarkable results: An easy & proven way to build good habits & break bad ones.* Avery, an imprint of Penguin Random House.

"Culture Definition & Meaning." (n.d.). *Merriam-Webster.* https://www.merriam-webster.com/dictionary/culture

"Culture Over Cash? Glassdoor Multi-Country Survey Finds More Than Half of Employees Prioritize Workplace Culture Over Salary." (2019, July 10). *Glassdoor.* https://www.glassdoor.com/about-us/workplace-culture-over-salary/

Forbes, H. T. (2013). *Help for Billy: A beyond consequences approach to helping children in the classroom.* Beyond Consequences Institute.

Grant, A. (2021). Building an anti-racist workplace transcript. *TED.* https://www.ted.com/podcasts/worklife/building-an-anti-racist-workplace-transcript

Herron, C. A., Dubreil, S., Cole, S. P., & Corrie, C. (2013). Using instructional video to teach culture to beginning foreign language students. *The CALICO Journal, 17,* 395-427.

Maxwell, J. C. (2020). *The leader's greatest return: Attracting, developing, and multiplying leaders.* [Kindle version]. HarperCollins Leadership. https://a.co/d/gfJOP8t

Peters, T., & Waterman, R. (1982). *In search of excellence: Lessons from America's best-run companies.* Harper Trade.

Solomon, L. (2016, March 9). Two-thirds of managers are uncomfortable communicating with employees. *Harvard Business Review.* https://hbr.org/2016/03/two-thirds-of-managers-are-uncomfortable-communicating-with-employees

X (Formerly Twitter). (n.d.). *x.com.* https://x.com/Joe_Sanfelippo/status/924254769811558400

CHAPTER 10
Identifying Core Values

"The values you and I live determine how we behave and how our culture will function – regardless of the laws we make."
~John C. Maxwell

The previous chapter analyzed the differences between organizational culture and climate and the extent to which leaders are responsible for establishing and supporting the overall environment. The purpose of this chapter is to take a deeper dive and understand how to identify and promote the core values that affect the prevailing climate and culture. In other words, what informs the daily actions, words, thoughts, and feelings that people use within an organization that ultimately contribute to how decisions are made and how it actually feels to live and work there?

For example, the culture of PreK-12 education in the United States is somewhat similar and predictable. Most schools start and finish their academic year at about the same time. The school day is similar, including how kids get to and from school, along with predictable patterns for breaks, events, and extra-curricular activities. However, just like understanding the difference between a country's culture and climate, one must actually spend time in a school's environment to understand the underlying reasons for how the predominant culture is carried out.

Figure 10.1: Culture, Climate, & Core Values

Furthermore, to truly understand why and how decisions are made in an organization, we must look at the core values that, for better or worse, are foundational to the overriding culture and climate. Just like we affect and are affected by culture and climate, regardless of our intentions, the same is true of core values – they exist and guide decisions and behavior *because of* or *in spite of* the clarity and intentionality of the organization's formal leadership.

In Chapter 9, you reflected upon the culture and climate of previous jobs, your current classroom, school, and district. As you work through this chapter, you might find it helpful to review these answers. In addition, similar to developing your personal mission statement, please take notes as you work through this chapter, as it will enable you to identify and reflect upon core values and related behaviors that are reflective of your leadership philosophy and overall character.

Finally, since this chapter is designed to be developmental, the questions and related activities can also be utilized when working in both small and large groups to better identify and determine the current and desired culture, climate, and core values.

Toxic Terrible Organization Award

When guiding groups and individual leaders in refining or clarifying their current and aspirational core values, I've found it effective to begin by identifying the opposite. Therefore, imagine that at the beginning of the school year, the State Board of Education decided it was going to give out the Toxic Terrible Organization Award to the most deserving school district. This award will be given at the end of the academic year. Since it's new, you have been asked to serve on a state-level committee responsible for developing the criteria, and you asked me to facilitate some of your group's discussions.

Although you weren't provided with many details, the liaison at the State Department shared that you must consider the following categories: actions, words, thoughts, and feelings. You were selected to be on this committee because, as a recognized teacher leader in your state, it's clear you do not work in a school district or organization that would qualify for this award. Accordingly, it's assumed that anything you contribute is due to your leadership acumen and not a reflection of your current professional environment.

Actions

As we have learned in previous chapters, success – or lack thereof – is intentionally defined on a daily basis and primarily driven by how people behave or are allowed to behave. Therefore, when thinking about the actions of an award-winning, toxic, terrible organization, consider the following questions:

- How are the organization's shared values, goals, and expectations conveyed through their actions? What are common actions that support this?
- How do people in this organization interact with colleagues and stakeholders?
- What are the underlying motivations for people's actions in this organization?
- What types of actions are encouraged, tolerated, allowed, and ignored?
- How do the prominent, daily actions make people feel both within and outside of the organization?

Based on your experiences and knowledge of organizational culture, are there other questions or criteria that should be added to provide a more complete picture of the actions that would be prevalent in this award-winning culture?

Words

When considering criteria for how the recipient of the Toxic Terrible Organization Award should demonstrate their use of words, we must be intentional and consider how these words can affect others. Once again, take time to answer the following questions:

- How are the organization's shared values, goals, and expectations conveyed through their words? What are examples of consistent and acceptable words, phrases, and messages?
- How do individuals within this organization use words with and about each other and also with external stakeholders? How are words used to treat others?
- What motivates people to consistently use and reinforce these words, phrases, and messages?
- What types of words, phrases, and messages are encouraged, tolerated, allowed, and ignored?
- How does the daily, accepted use of these words, phrases, and messages make people feel both within and outside of the organization?

Thoughts

Based on the types of actions and words that would be prevalent in this Toxic Terrible Organization, what types of thoughts would this typically evoke? While identifying or predicting people's thoughts isn't an exact science, from an organizational standpoint, it is possible to sense underlying and consistent themes and narratives. Therefore, analyze the following:

- How do people in this organization think about themselves, their colleagues, those they serve, and stakeholders?
- What are some of the constant narratives or stories that exist within this organization that are related to and inform people's actions, words, and thoughts?
- If asked to share their thoughts about their levels of job satisfaction and engagement with the organization, how would people respond?
- Is it possible to identify one or two overarching thoughts or narratives that capture the essence of what it means to live and work in this organization? If so, what would they be?
- What types of thoughts, stories, or gossip are prevalent in this organization?
- Who are the primary thought leaders or storytellers, and why are their thoughts and stories encouraged?
- For whom are the primary thoughts, stories, and narratives helpful and harmful?
- If asked their overall thoughts about the organizational environment, how would stakeholders respond?

Feelings

If you recall from previous chapters, determining how it feels to live and work in an organization on a daily basis not only provides insight into its culture but is also a powerful indicator of the core values that inform decisions and encourage prevailing actions, words, and thoughts. Therefore, as we consider this category of requirements and qualifications for the Toxic Terrible Organization Award, please answer the following:

- On a daily basis, how does it feel to live in this organization based upon what's encouraged, tolerated, allowed, and ignored?

- What do people tend to look forward to, and what do they avoid or dread?
- What feelings influence people's behavior and actions?
- How do stakeholders feel about this organization?
- How do people who work here feel about returning to this organization at the start of each week?

Toxic Terrible Category Descriptions

Now that we have explored the four main categories and addressed questions that will provide additional insight into the type of culture and climate that would be worthy of this award let's assume we have analyzed the data, summarized our responses and thoughts, and have come up with the following to serve as the first draft of the award selection criteria.

Actions

The organization promotes a lack of respect through tolerating rude, dismissive, or undermining behavior. Individuals often ignore boundaries with aggressive competition encouraged over collaboration. Leaders model dismissive behaviors, leading to actions of disrespect and apathy.

Words

Words are used to complain, blame-shift, and make excuses, contributing to a negative environment of fear and defensiveness. Phrases like "not my fault" and "that's just how it is" are common, further contributing to a narrative of stagnation and resentment.

Thoughts

Most members of the organization think in terms of self-preservation due to a lack of trust. Gossip is prevalent, and individuals are quick to question each other's motives, always assuming negative intentions. These thoughts promote a "watch your back" mentality, which perpetuates the toxic narrative.

Feelings
People feel constant anxiety and lack motivation to engage. Daily experiences are filled with dread, with little anticipation or hope for positive change. Overall, people feel isolated and unsupported, leading to high stress and low morale.

Toxic Terrible Core Values
As a result of these descriptions, the following core values emerged, which the selection committee felt were adequate representations of an award-winning, toxic, terrible organization.

Anxiety and Frustration
Those working in this organization experience persistent stress due to unclear expectations, lack of support, and a toxic climate devoid of growth, fulfillment, and satisfaction.

Apathy and Isolation
There is a lack of engagement and connection, where people feel unsupported and unmotivated, leading to disengagement and minimal collaboration and overall connection to the organization.

Blame and Excuses
Avoiding responsibility by shifting blame onto others and making excuses is commonplace, thus creating a climate of defensiveness and mistrust.

Disrespect
A lack of regard for others' contributions, ideas, and boundaries, with rude or dismissive behavior is tolerated and even encouraged.

Distrust and Control

People are quick to question each other's motives, always assuming negative intentions, thus resulting in a controlling, "protect your own" mentality.

Inconsistency
Standards and policies are applied unevenly, creating confusion, frustration, and a lack of clarity and accountability.

Negative Talk
Words are used as weapons. Complaints, gossip, innuendo, whisper campaigns, and discouraging language are pervasive, eroding morale and creating a pessimistic climate.

Remember, leadership is a day job shaped by our daily decisions, behaviors, words, and actions. Accordingly, the overriding core values created, permitted, and promoted by an organization's formal leaders serve as the guiding principles – one conversation, behavior, action, or feeling at a time. If we look at the actual culture of an organization, the core values become apparent, and we can also somewhat predict future behavior.

For example, if you were to enter a school building you are unfamiliar with and were told a core value is blaming others and making excuses, how do you think the faculty will respond when the state assessment data are released and the results are less than favorable for their students? Additionally, how do you think people will interact with one another and use words? Will they be used to build up and encourage or tear down and demean? Most likely, it will be consistent with their core values.

The B.E.S.T. Organization Award

Now let's move on from discussing the characteristics and traits of a negative organization and look at how to identify and develop positive core values or what I like to call your B.E.S.T. organization, which stands for the following:

Behaviors (Actions)

Emotions (Feelings)

Stories (Thoughts)

Treatment (Words)

I must admit that I intentionally started this chapter and subsequent activities using the categories of *actions, feelings, thoughts*, and *words* because they're relevant to an organization's culture, climate, and core values, and are also more linguistically effective when thinking about a toxic, terrible award! Nonetheless, since the goal of this chapter and the book as a whole is to add value to you and those you serve by helping you uncover and enhance your inherent leadership abilities, which is a positive endeavor, using the B.E.S.T. acronym is understandably more uplifting and still aligns with our purpose.

Figure 10.2: B.E.S.T. Core Values

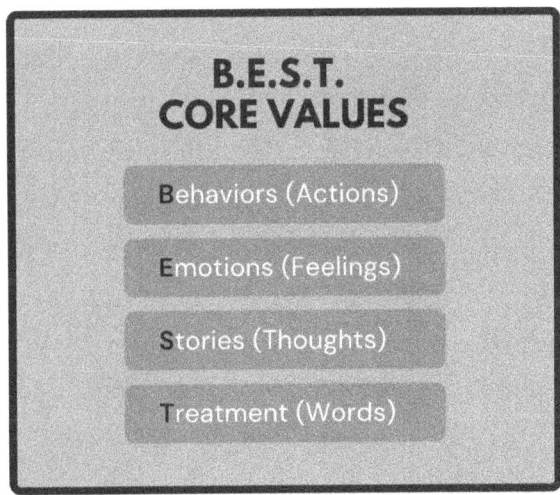

To flip the script on the previous activity, imagine you are now responsible for developing the criteria for the B.E.S.T. Organization Award, and while you are still free to draw upon your leadership expertise, you may now talk about and support your own building or district along with referencing and recommending previous places you have taught! Once again, please consider the following questions for each of the four required categories, realizing that you already display and promote many of these characteristics and values within your own classroom and as you work with colleagues and stakeholders in your building, district, and community.

Finally, because this activity could realistically be conducted within your own school or district with your colleagues, the targeted questions are slightly modified from the Toxic Terrible activity. Take time to analyze, answer, and reflect upon the following questions within each of the four categories.

Behaviors
- What types of behaviors are indicative of and support the values, goals, and expectations of the organization?
- What are some specific behaviors that intentionally and frequently happen within this organization that reflect the prevailing culture and climate?
- Give examples of behaviors that are encouraged, tolerated, allowed, and ignored.
- If asked, how would stakeholders describe the predominant behaviors within this organization?
- How do these behaviors make others feel? What does it enable them to do, accomplish, and become?

Emotions
- Based upon the behaviors and values that are encouraged, tolerated, allowed, and ignored, how does it feel to be a part

of this organization on a daily basis? What are some of the prominent feelings among those inside and outside of the organization?
- Describe the emotions and feelings expressed when people in this organization are asked to collaborate or support each other.
- What are some of the emotions and feelings expressed when the formal leaders/administrators interact with people inside and outside of the organization?
- What primary and predominant emotions play a role in driving people's behaviors and actions within the organization?
- How would most people within the organization describe their emotions and feelings when thinking about and preparing for another week of work?

Stories
- If asked about their thoughts, opinions, and connections to the overall culture and climate, what types of stories, narratives, or self-talk would be prevalent among those who work in the organization?
- What types of stories, narratives, or self-talk are encouraged, tolerated, allowed, and ignored on a daily basis?
- Who are the primary thought leaders or storytellers within the organization, and why?
- What are one or two commonly accepted stories or narratives that adequately illustrate what it means (and how it feels) to live and work in this organization?
- When confronted with challenges or times of crisis, what are common stories, narratives, and thoughts that emerge among those within the organization, including the formal leaders?

Treatment
- How are the predominant shared values, goals, and expectations reflected in how people treat each other, both within and outside of the organization?
- If a qualified colleague was interested in applying for a position in this organization and asked you how they would be treated, what would you tell them?
- What are specific examples of the type of treatment that is encouraged, tolerated, allowed, and ignored on a daily basis?
- To what extent does the prevailing, daily treatment within this organization contribute to how it feels to live and work there?
- What does the consistent and accepted manner of treatment within this organization enable or cause people (internally and externally) to do, accomplish, and become?

B.E.S.T. Category Descriptions

Once again, let's assume we have analyzed the data generated from the application questions based on the four categories and have developed the following descriptions to assist us in the review process, keeping in mind that we are now considering healthy, vibrant, and supportive organizations.

Behaviors

In these organizations, behaviors demonstrate and promote mutual respect on a daily basis through positive interactions, active listening, consistently following through on responsibilities, providing constructive feedback, and creating a supportive, accountable culture and climate. In addition, actions and behaviors make it socially acceptable to set and respect healthy, realistic boundaries for yourself and others.

Emotions

In healthy organizations, predominant, consistent feelings and emotions reinforce the positive environment and include but are not limited to enthusiasm, joy, pride, commitment, ownership, and belonging. Individuals feel compelled to collaborate with and support each other, including external stakeholders. An abundance mentality is prevalent; success is viewed as an infinite resource that is to be shared throughout the organization.

Stories

The predominant stories, narratives, and self-talk support the positive values, experiences, and expectations of the organization and are reflective of team success, resiliency, innovation, and having the space and agency to make mistakes, try again, and ultimately improve.

Treatment

People treat themselves and each other (inside and outside of the organization) with kindness. They assume positive intent, show appreciation, and are open and transparent with their communication. Words are used to build people up and support them, thus reflecting a message of inclusion and acceptance.

B.E.S.T. Core Values

After agreeing upon the previous category descriptions, the following core values emerged that are also reflective of healthy cultures, climates, and organizations.

Accountability

Individuals understand and take responsibility for their actions and associated outcomes, including how their behavior and words might affect others. Holding each other accountable isn't seen as punitive but is understood to be supportive and developmental.

Belonging
Individuals feel a sense of belonging because they are valued, seen, heard, and appreciated. The default decision is to include, not exclude, others.

Growth
People understand that growth and change are a natural part of evolving to serve others. Accordingly, the organization embraces a growth mindset, acknowledging the need for continued personal and professional development. This also includes resiliency and the ability to grow and adapt, especially during times of unforeseen change or crisis.

Integrity
All actions, decisions, behaviors, words, and treatment are grounded in being honest and maintaining strong ethical standards, both within and outside of the organization.

Respect
Each person is respected both personally and professionally, and their contributions to the organization are acknowledged and valued.

Once again, let's consider the example used with the Toxic Terrible Core Values to see the difference. Now, if you were to enter a B.E.S.T. Award school and be told that one of their core values is accountability, how do you think this group of staffulty and stakeholders would respond to less than favorable state test results? Additionally, how do you think people would feel, interact with, and treat one another?

To further illustrate, apply, and understand the significance that core values play within an organization, please review and reflect upon the following Core Values Application Scenarios, noting how, based on the culture, climate, and core values within an organization, people can respond differently to the same situation.

Core Values Application Scenario #1

A teacher notices their colleague's lesson plan doesn't align with the standards the grade-level team agreed upon.

Toxic Terrible Reaction
Actions
The teacher criticizes their partner to others, saying, "They never follow through."

Words
They avoid direct communication, blaming them for team challenges and failures.

Feelings
Frustration and annoyance build, leading to gossip, resentment, and division.

Toxic Terrible Core Value
Disrespect

B.E.S.T. Reaction
Behaviors
The teacher discusses the issue privately, offering support and resources to help align with team standards.

Treatment
They say, "How can I help support you? I know you can do it."

Emotions
Respect and support build between team members, creating trust and connection.

B.E.S.T. Core Values
Accountability and respect.

Core Values Application Scenario #2
A teacher wins a district-level award for teaching excellence.

Toxic Terrible Reaction
Thoughts
Colleagues feel resentment, believing favoritism or politics was involved.

Words
They downplay the award, saying, "They just got it because of who they know. I've seen them teach, and I could do better."

Feelings
Envy, resentment, and frustration arise, creating division.

Toxic Terrible Core Values
Distrust and control.

B.E.S.T. Reaction
Behaviors
Colleagues congratulate the teacher, acknowledging their hard work.

Treatment
They say, "Congratulations! We're so proud of you!"

Emotions
Positive feelings, such as pride, contribute to team cohesiveness and enhance morale, thus inspiring others.

B.E.S.T. Core Values
Belonging and respect.

Core Values Application Scenario #3

A building principal learns about the benefits of implementing a teacher leadership program in their district and presents it to their faculty.

Toxic Terrible Reaction

Thoughts

Teachers react skeptically, assuming it's one more thing on their plates without support.

Words

Comments such as, "Just another initiative that'll go nowhere." "I'm too busy to worry about these ivory tower ideas that claim to help students and make me a better teacher."

Feelings

Resistance builds, viewing the program as another task with no personal benefit to self and students.

Toxic Terrible Core Values

Apathy and isolation.

B.E.S.T. Reaction

Behaviors

Teachers show interest, asking questions about how they can contribute and learn more.

Treatment

They say, "How can we get involved and make this successful?" "Sounds like it helps students and might make me a better teacher and leader!"

Emotions

Excitement and motivation foster a sense of shared purpose and opportunity for growth.

B.E.S.T. Core Values
Growth and integrity.

As a final activity, go through each of the previous three scenarios again, and determine if there are other core values represented by each of the two organizations. Additionally, look at the cumulative reactions to the scenarios within each organization and say, "That's how they do things there." Yes, actually say it out loud because it's true! Likewise, look at the B.E.S.T reactions to each scenario, and in addition to acknowledging "That's how they do things there," also imagine them responding the same way the Toxic Terrible organization did and say, *"That's not how they do things there!"*

Discussion and Application Questions

1. Think of a scenario in which two schools would have a similar culture and climate but different core values. In what ways might they respond differently to the same scenario?

2. Thinking about your own classroom, what are three to five core values you currently (or hope to) follow? What can you do on a daily basis to reinforce or enhance these core values?

3. What are your experiences working in organizations that had either a positive or negative culture, climate, and related core values? What lessons will you take away from this and apply to your current classroom and potential leadership roles in the future?

CHAPTER 11

Addressing Conflict with Courage, Comfort, and Consistency

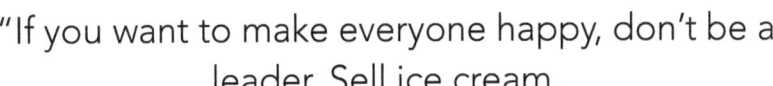

"If you want to make everyone happy, don't be a leader. Sell ice cream.
~Nick Saban

How do you feel about conflict? If you could create the perfect day at school, would it include being involved with or addressing any form of conflict? If you are like most people in the world, I'm fairly confident you would prefer not to deal with it, which is understandable. In fact, I would be concerned if you said your perfect day – in or outside of school – would only be complete if it included conflict and drama.

Let me ask you another question. Before you officially became a teacher and had your own classroom, what were some of your biggest fears? Having spent considerable time training future teachers, I would guess classroom management was at the top of your list, which is common. Why? Because effective classroom management – or let's call it what it really is, *classroom leadership* – means you're in the people business. And as we know, people can be messy and unpredictable.

Therefore, while most new teachers are comfortable with some of the more predictable variables of the profession – like content, standards, and assessments – it's the developing humans for whom we show up each day that can cause some initial anxiety. In other words, most new and beginning teachers are nervous about entering the classroom because they're aware that effective classroom leadership requires addressing conflict on a daily basis. Here's the good news! Eventually, most teachers become very comfortable addressing many types of conflict, oftentimes doing so without realizing it.

As we've learned in previous chapters, one of the reasons teachers are hesitant to pursue both formal and informal leadership roles outside of the classroom is because they are concerned about addressing conflict among other adults such as colleagues, parents, and stakeholders.

As I have also mentioned in previous chapters, I have been teaching the concepts in this book to both future and current teachers for a number of years, both in formal classroom settings and through workshops, professional development, speaking, and coaching. While I initially assumed that using non-classroom conflict scenarios (i.e., colleague and colleague) would be the most effective way to teach these concepts, it was suggested by a few experienced teachers that we instead bridge the gap by using scenarios based within the classroom but involve teachers having the difficult conversation with other adults, such as students' parents. This has proven to be successful because part of being a classroom teacher is addressing parent conflict, and in addition, the concepts we will learn can be adapted to other forms of adult conflict, such as between two colleagues.

Understanding Conflict

When you hear the word conflict, what ideas and feelings emerge? According to *Dictionary.com*, conflict can be defined as "incompatibility or interference, as of one idea, desire, event, or activity with another" (n.d.). Using this definition, can you think about a time in your personal or professional life in which you had a conflict – usually with one or more people – that was due to some type of incompatibility or interference of ideas or desires? To what extent was this conflict exacerbated due to a lack of communication or people telling themselves stories that simply were not true? Did you and others view this as a competition in which there had to be a clear winner and loser? If so, what were the criteria, rules of the game, scorecard, or standards by which the winner was determined? (Hint: while it's human nature and we're all guilty of wanting to win a conflict, the truth is that either both parties win or both parties lose because it's not a game or competition.)

Think about your first year as a teacher – or list things you are currently concerned about if you are a future teacher. What were some of the specific scenarios or behaviors you were concerned about addressing in the classroom? While I'm sure some of these may have emerged, others didn't, and of course, new things popped up you could not have predicted, I'd bet you are now much more confident and proficient in addressing these scenarios and behaviors, which most likely represent some form of conflict.

For example, it's possible you learned early on that once an issue arises in your classroom you have two choices: address it immediately or ignore it. Furthermore, if you're like most new teachers with the best of intentions, including me, perhaps you thought ignoring the problem would cause it to go away, thus making the decision to accept temporary comfort over long-term success. However, I'm sure you quickly learned a powerful principle of leadership: *problems, if ignored, never truly go away but, instead, continue to grow each day.* As you are keenly aware, in the life of a classroom teacher, problems that aren't addressed immediately can be the gift that keeps on giving and will continue for the rest of the school year.

One thing all teachers understand is the importance of proper planning. Granted, even the best of plans can take a few unexpected turns when implemented in the real world, but in the end, our classes and daily schedules are usually more effective and efficient when we start with a sound plan. The same is true for addressing conflict, especially as it pertains to influencing others, such as colleagues, parents, and stakeholders. Just like we try to begin each class with some type of lesson plan or road map, the same is true for effectively preparing for a conflict-based scenario.

Similar to planning an instructional unit, when I organized the scope and sequence of the chapters in this book, I was intentional about waiting to discuss conflict toward the end. This was primarily because of its importance and how most people react to it. I wanted to address your levels of concern by first providing the foundational tools, reflections, and conceptual framework through the Professional Educator Mission Statement, A Leader's Daily Five, H.A.B.I.T.S., and the leadership principles of service, character, courage, and relationships.

Preparing for Conflict

Since we know that some form of conflict happens daily in the life of a leader and we must address it before it grows and produces more problems, the following pre-conflict checklist can be helpful. What follows is most effective in the event you can foresee or have some advance notice of a conflict (such as engaging in a difficult conversation). However, going through this activity can also better prepare you for conflict scenarios for which there is little to no warning.

Pre-Conflict Checklist
- Whom do you serve?
- Have you built relationships?
- Do your homework.
- Transpose the problem.
- Reflect your culture, climate, and core values.
- Choose courage and rationalize your fear.

Whom Do You Serve?
As you prepare to address conflict, remind yourself of why you serve and influence others as a professional educator. Think about the Professional Educator Mission Statement you

developed in Chapter 6, which most likely indicates why you do what you do and for whom you do it – your students.

While I'm sure you understand how your interactions with students in the classroom, building, and district align with your mission to teach kids, have you ever thought about the inherent advocacy role you play as a professional educator? Serving students also means being a positive professional advocate who influences and supports other teachers, administrators, parents, and stakeholders. In addition, as previously mentioned, a conflict is not a competition but rather a way to serve others, renegotiate the terms of professional relationships, and ultimately move your organization – and its ability to serve students – forward.

Therefore, it's important to realize that the one person you are *not serving* when you engage in a conflict is yourself. Remember from the Teacher-Leader's Credo that "It starts with me but isn't about me." Accordingly, prior to engaging in any type of conflict with another person, remember that doing so is not only part of your professional role and responsibility but also serves as a form of advocacy for your students.

Have You Built Relationships?

As a classroom teacher, you clearly understand the importance of building relationships and how that can positively impact the instances where you have to reinforce expectations, have a tough conversation, or simply be the adult in the room. In fact, a core principle of leadership – in any field – is realizing we all carry a relational equity account with those we serve and will eventually need to make a withdrawal. The extent to which we have previously built a relationship with that other person will determine if a conflict-based interaction keeps our account in the black or the red. Simply stated, engaging in a tough conversation with another person, be it a student, colleague, or parent, means we have to spend some of the relational equity we have previously established with them.

While we obviously can't ensure we have a solid and robust relational equity account with every person with whom we will interact, it is possible to be intentional with our daily actions to ensure we are making the best possible effort. Again, as a teacher, you are like a 24/7 billboard for who you are, what you believe, and how you make others feel.

Accordingly, prior to a conflict scenario, think about whether or not you have already built a strong relationship with the other person. If you haven't, what do you know about them and their reputation either as a professional colleague or someone outside of your school? Do they tend to be negative, abrasive, or perpetually perturbed? Are they perceived to be a strong advocate and a generally positive person? How have they reacted in previous conversations you or your colleagues have had with them?

Although you certainly cannot predict with 100% accuracy how the other person will respond, simply being aware of the fact that this is part of your relationship journey (and future history) with this person can provide the proper mindset as you prepare. Remember, you are not just having a tough conversation or delivering undesirable news; you are either continuing, initiating, or renegotiating a relationship with another person that will ultimately build or lose equity.

Do Your Homework
Conflict involves context, and there are always multiple variables and versions of a story, even if it may not initially appear that way. Therefore, before engaging in conflict, gather all relevant information – emails, documentation, policies, or agreements – and attempt to understand the big picture. For

instance, if the conflict involves a parent upset about grading, review your class documents, grading criteria, and any prior communication to ensure you're prepared to address concerns fairly and transparently.

Doing your homework also means anticipating questions and potential misunderstandings. As we will learn later in this chapter, taking the time to script key points or role-play the conversation with a trusted colleague can be helpful in removing any personal feelings or biases you have going into the scenario. (Please ensure that when you role-play, you are not sharing confidential or identifying information.)

Transpose the Problem

Another way to adequately prepare for conflict that will help you maintain fairness and remove bias is to transpose the problem and the person. For example, if you have been teaching for any length of time and I were to ask you, "Who is most likely to do this unacceptable thing in your classroom or school?" you could easily come up with a few names. This doesn't mean they're bad kids; it just means you know your kids. You know their idiosyncrasies and quirks and could guess which one would be most likely to do something ornery that gets under your skin. And while I know you still engage with these kids in a positive and constructive manner, being human means you're probably not too surprised when it happens and might have a slight bias, telling yourself, "I knew they would do this." "Why does it always have to be *this* kiddo?"

Likewise, you could also list the kids least likely to be the culprits of unacceptable actions and behaviors. Again, this doesn't mean you play favorites, it just means you know your kids, who are still developing humans. Additionally, if you're being honest, I'd bet you would feel more disappointed if the least likely kids did something out of character and, as a result, you might approach the ensuing conversation differently. (I'm sure you can also think of colleagues, parents, or community members who would be most or least likely to behave a certain way.)

Transposing the problem – in any conflict scenario – means the story you are telling yourself is that the person with whom you will interact is the *least likely person* to have done the alleged action or behavior. I know this might be the third time in two weeks you have had to address this same issue, but again, be the bigger person, be the best professional you can be, and *assume positive intent.* Transpose the problem and approach it from the standpoint of "I'm disappointed in the behavior, but I'm seeking resolution, not *restitution.*"

Reflect Your Culture, Climate, and Core Values
In my experience training and coaching PreK-12 and higher education leaders, especially as they start their first formal leadership job, I always tell them that it's possible to quantify the distance between the culture they inherited and the culture they want to promote by the number of difficult conversations they're willing to have. This is because all great leaders understand that culture, climate, and core values are established and promoted one conversation, interaction, and relationship at a time.

Again, you inherently understand this leadership concept. For example, why do you, as an effective classroom teacher, spend a significant amount of time in the first few days of school (shout out to Harry Wong) intentionally teaching your kids how things are done in your classroom? It's because you know that's how to establish and promote your culture, climate, and core values. If you want kids to feel safe and respected, you must spend time teaching and modeling the core value of "We don't use words to hurt people." Furthermore, if you start the year with a few kids who need additional reminders of how things are done in your classroom, you have essentially identified the number of conversations (interactions and relationships) it will take to achieve your desired culture.

Therefore, I encourage you to realize that the same tactics you use for your own classroom and students are applicable when leading adults through negotiating conflict. Refer to your mission statement from Chapter 6. What values do you want others to see in you? How do you want them to feel? What do you want them to be able to do, become, and accomplish as a result of your influence? Remember, being the CEO of your classroom doesn't stop at the classroom door. You always promote who you are as a professional in your school, district, and community.

Accordingly, remind yourself of your prevailing culture, climate, and core values. Write them down as you prepare to have a difficult conversation with another person and think about the supporting words and behaviors. For example, if you have transposed the problem to where you would naturally assume positive intent because you want everyone to feel valued, seen, and heard, then you need to use words and actions that reflect this core value when engaging in conflict with others, both inside and outside of your classroom.

Choose Courage and Rationalize Your Fear
Addressing conflict requires both courage and clarity. As a human being, it's natural to feel uncomfortable stepping into difficult conversations – whether it's resolving a misunderstanding with a parent or navigating tension with a colleague. Avoiding these situations might seem easier in the short term, but as we know, unresolved issues only continue to grow. Choosing to confront conflict demonstrates

accountability and advocacy, but doing so starts with understanding and rationalizing your fear.

Fear often stems from concerns about damaging relationships, appearing confrontational, or being misunderstood. This is also frequently made worse by the stories and assumptions we tell ourselves, most of which are untrue and rarely materialize. Accordingly, as you approach a conflict scenario, acknowledge these stories and fears and ask yourself the following questions:

- Is the story I'm telling myself true?
- If so, what evidence do I have to support this?
- What am I truly afraid of, and what's the worst that could happen?

By addressing these concerns, you can eliminate unwarranted fears, remove natural bias, and lean into your courage, thus focusing on resolving the issue at hand while being professional and fair. As Brené Brown (2019) suggests, adopt a mindset in which you seek to "get it right" as opposed to "being right" (p. 92).

A final note on preparing for and addressing conflict. While it should be implied, I need to mention that you should always check with your administration before engaging in conflict to ensure you're not running up against policies, protocol, or potential political or legal issues. Assuming you are not, which is often the case, the following provides an effective template.

"Likes" Template for Addressing Conflict

Although conflict can come in many forms, addressing it usually involves having a conversation with another person in which you try to negotiate a mutual understanding and agreed-upon outcome. In the book *Never Split the Difference: Negotiating* as *If Your Life Depended on It*, former FBI hostage negotiator Christopher Voss and co-author Tahl Raz (2016) provide an excellent and in-depth framework for the art of negotiation. The good news is it's highly unlikely that most of us will have to engage in a high-stakes hostage negotiation. However, I have found that adapting some of the negotiation strategies either suggested or inspired by the work of Voss and Raz can be applicable to almost any type of conflict, especially within an educational setting.

The following are the steps involved in planning and preparing for various kinds of conflict, such as difficult conversations or negotiations. I refer to this as the Conflict "Likes" Template since each step is characterized by a phrase using the word like:

- Step 1: Summarize and Set the Stage
    - What's happened?
    - What would **I like** the outcome to be?
    - Here's what I'm hopeful we can accomplish together.
- Step 2: Anticipate and Address
    - It probably **seems like**...
- Step 3: Repeat and Reinforce
    - It **sounds like**...
- Step 4: Find the Fix
    - What does fixed **look like**?
- Step 5: Listen and Lean In
    - What would **you like** to see?
- Step 6: Collaborate and Commit
    - What would **we both like** to see?

To help reinforce and operationalize these steps, we will use this scenario and provide examples:

A parent of one of your students has contacted you, suggesting the only reason their kid is failing your class is because you "have it out for their kid" and "are just a bad teacher." The parent has requested a meeting with you to talk about their kid's grades, assuming it's your fault. However, what the parent doesn't realize is that you have been working a great deal with this student, and despite your best efforts to contact the parent, they will not reply.

Step 1: Summarize and Set the Stage

Start by answering the question, "What's happened?" To do this, summarize the situation that has led to the conflict based on tangible, documented evidence along with associated protocols, policies, and rules. This is part of doing your homework! Take the time to objectively analyze the previous behaviors, conversations, and consequences that have already been implemented and, if possible, the extent to which there might be infractions of stated policies. Doing so will not only allow you to step back and analyze the situation from a more neutral perspective but might also reveal some of your own missteps in terms of unintentional bias or simply being too emotionally connected.

Table 11.1: Step 1, Question 1

Step 1: Summarize and Set the Stage Q1: "What's happened?"
- The student has consistently submitted incomplete work and displayed either a combative or apathetic attitude towards improving their academic performance.
- The student has not presented any behaviors that warrant their removal from my class, but I have tried to visit with them one-on-one, expressing my belief in their abilities and offering assistance with assignments.

Step 1: Summarize and Set the Stage Q1: "What's happened?"
- Per district protocol, I update my grades regularly which means the parent has the opportunity to receive notifications through the approved program or app on their phone.
- Per district protocol, I have regularly sent emails to the parent – their preferred mode of communication – but have not received a reply.
- I have asked the student if their parent has mentioned receiving my emails because I want to be supportive and help them succeed, and the student usually says something to the effect of "Yeah. My mom got those, but she's fine if I fail."

Similar to utilizing backward design when planning an instructional unit, begin with the end in mind and ask yourself, *"What would I like the outcome to be?"* Remember to focus on getting it right instead of being right and consider the following:

- Define your ideal outcome.
- Consider what success looks like for both parties.
- Write down a specific, realistic goal.

Table 11.2 Step 1, Question 2

Step 1: Summarize and Set the Stage Q2: "What would I like the outcome to be?"
I would like the parent to know I care about their child, I know they have the potential to be successful in my class, and I truly want to develop a plan to ensure the parent is aware of their student's performance. I want the parent to know I am willing to work with them to support their child.

Finally, based on the previous steps and your stated goal, complete the following lead-off phrase, which you could actually use at the start of the conversation to set the stage for a collaborative effort: *"Here's what I'm hopeful we can accomplish together..."*

Table 11.3: Step 1, Question 3

Step 1: Summarize and Set the Stage Q3: "Here's what I'm hopeful we can accomplish together..."
I'm hopeful we can work together to support your child's success. I believe they have the potential to do well, and I want to keep you informed about their progress so we can create a plan that will help them be successful.

Please note that when you answer the questions in this step, say and answer them out loud. This might seem a bit odd or uncomfortable, but there's something about putting the words out there and forcing ourselves to answer them in real-time that has a way of either reinforcing their validity or revealing their flaws.

Step 2: Anticipate and Address

Let's be honest. Most normal humans go into a conflict scenario with a bit of anxiety and perhaps resentment that the other person said something, engaged in a behavior, or failed to do something that has led to a disagreement. If you recall from a previous chapter, I shared that early in my teaching career I learned the value of saying *the second thing* that came to my mind when I was addressing student behavior in real time and was probably too emotionally invested.

In this step, we actually anticipate the *first things* other people are feeling or telling themselves about us, the school, community, policies, etc., and address them head-on in a way that is constructive and can help clear the air. Voss and Raz (2016) refer to this process as "labeling," which is a way to identify someone's feelings, turn them into words, and then very calmly and respectfully repeat their feelings and emotions back to them (p. 54).

To do this, think about the other person's negative thoughts or accusations and turn them into an *"It seems like..."* statement. From personal experience, I have found inserting the word "probably" or "might" can help soften the accusation, so instead of saying "It seems like you think I don't like your kid," "It probably seems like I don't like your kid," or "It might seem like I don't like your kid," opens the door for them to respond honestly without feeling directly threatened.

In the Anticipate and Address step, there are two ways to utilize an "It seems like" statement. The first is by addressing the elephant in the room and turning the negative and most likely untrue things they're thinking about you into a direct statement such as, *"It probably seems like I'm a terrible teacher,"* which gives them the chance to either openly deny it or indicate you need to spend some time addressing the concern. The following table provides a few examples of how this might occur in our given scenario.

Table 11.4: Step 2a

Step 2a: Anticipate and Address "It probably seems like..."	
Potential Thoughts or Concerns	"It probably seems like" Statement
The parent thinks I have it out for their kid.	*It probably seems like I'm a terrible teacher who doesn't like your kid.*
The parent believes I don't want their kid to succeed in my class.	*It probably seems like I don't want your kids to be successful in my class.*
The parent believes I have not made the effort to contact them about their kid's grades.	*It probably seems like I don't prioritize communicating with parents.*

The second way to utilize an "It seems like" statement in the Anticipate and Address step is as an initial way to signal you and the other person agree on something and are actually on the same page and most likely will want to work together towards a solution, such as *"It seems like you care about your child's success in my class."* In the following table, notice how the "It probably seems like" statement from Step 2a can then be converted into "It seems like" statements that attempt to allow the other person to acknowledge their ideas or concerns in a way that will ultimately show the two of you share that opinion.

Table 11.5: Step 2b

Step 2b: Anticipate and Address "It seems like…"	
Initial "Probably seems like" Statement	"It seems like…"
It probably seems like I'm a terrible teacher who doesn't like your kid.	It seems like you recognize the value of great teachers.
It might seem like I don't want your kid to be successful in my class.	It seems like you care about your child's academic success.
It probably seems like I don't prioritize communicating with parents.	It seems like you value updated communication about your child's schoolwork.

Voss and Raz (2016) offer additional examples of "It seems like" statements below:

- *It seems like _____ is valuable to you.*
- *It seems like you don't like_____.*
- *It seems like you value_____.*
- *It seems like _____ makes it easier.*
- *It seems like you're reluctant to_____.*

- It seems like _____ is important.
- It seems you are worried that_____. (p. 254)

You might be thinking this all sounds great, but how does it look in real-time, especially if they agree and feel like you really are a terrible teacher? The following dialog should provide some clarity:

> **Teacher:** Hi, Parent, I'm so glad we were able to connect to find a way to support Your Child's learning and success in my class. I understand there's been some confusion and perhaps a glitch in our communication. It probably seems like I'm just a terrible teacher who doesn't care if your child is successful.
>
> **Parent Response A:** No, I don't think you're a terrible teacher, but I am upset that you haven't reached out to me and that my kid says you aren't willing to help them in class....
>
> **Teacher Response A:** Thank you – I do care about all of my students. It sounds like ensuring consistent communication and helping your child in my class is important to you. To be honest, I have... (list the attempted communication, efforts to help the child, etc.) but certainly understand if you were unaware of these efforts. It seems like you care about your child's academic success.
>
> **Parent Response B:** You're right! I think you're a terrible teacher. You won't call or email me about my kid, and all I hear is that you just ignore them and won't do anything to help.
>
> **Teacher Response B:** I appreciate your honesty and want to assure you that I care deeply about all of my

students. While I understand your frustration, to be honest, I have... (list the attempted communication, efforts to help the child, etc.) *but certainly understand if you were unaware of these efforts. It seems like you care about your child's academic success.*

Step 3: Repeat and Reinforce

Step 3 represents the first attempt to move to the same side of the table, thus opening up the dialog to ultimately find a solution moving forward. Based on the responses and information gained in Step 2, this step reminds us that we need to continue to listen to the other person to better understand the story they are telling themselves. To do this, we must repeat and reinforce their stated concerns and assumptions, using the phrase, "It sounds like."

While there may not appear to be a significant difference, saying "sounds like" as opposed to "seems like" shows you are seeing, hearing, and understanding the other person based on what they have shared with you (you are repeating their thoughts and concerns). In the table below, notice how this is based on the previous steps and uses the pronoun "we" to show a mutual understanding and common goal.

Table 11. 6: Step 3

Step 3: Repeat and Reinforce *"It sounds like..."*
"It sounds like we both value effective teachers."
"It sounds like we both care about your child's academic success."
"It sounds like we both agree that we need to communicate to support your child."

Step 4: Find the Fix

After removing some barriers, addressing false assumptions and narratives, and verbalizing that you and the other person value the same things, you can now take a let's-fix-this-together-approach, and directly ask them, "*What does fixed look like?*" Using this question serves two primary purposes when involved in a conflict scenario.

Asking "What does fixed look like?" gets right to the point and, in a positive and assertive manner, essentially asks the other person, "What do you want?" For example, the teacher could say "*Since it sounds like we both want your child to be successful in my class, what does fixed look like to you?*" As we will see in the next steps, this opens the door to both parties working together to reach a reasonable solution.

In addition, "What does fixed look like?" can also be used to re-direct the conversation and help everyone focus on the task at hand in the event they become unreasonable, emotional, or simply get sidetracked from the conversation. While most effective after the first three steps (Summarize and Set the Stage, Anticipate and Address, and Repeat and Reinforce), this phrase can be used at any time in the conversation, similar to calling a time out or requesting a break. When used in our previous scenario, it's helpful to add the phrase "*in a perfect world.*" For example, let's continue the previous dialog from Step 3.

> **Teacher:** *I appreciate your honesty and want to assure you that I care deeply about all of my students. While I understand your frustration, to be honest, I have...* (list the attempted communication, efforts to help the child, etc.) *but certainly understand if you were unaware of these efforts. It seems like you care about your child's academic success.*

> **Parent:** That's cute! I'm sure you always say that to everyone. Doesn't change the fact that my kid is failing your class.
>
> **Teacher:** Look, I really want to work with you and support your kid here, so can you just tell me, in a perfect world, what does fixed look like to you?

While adding "in a perfect world" might seem insignificant, it will either force the other person to think somewhat realistically in terms of what can actually occur or, if they are unable to do this, it gives you the perfect opportunity to address it, using what Voss and Raz (2016) refer to as the "greatest-of-all-time-calibrated question: "How am I supposed to do that?" (p. 151). I then suggest following up with a "Do you realize if…" statement.

> **Teacher:** Look, I really want to work with you and support your kid here, so can you just tell me, in a perfect world, what does fixed look like to you?
>
> **Parent:** I want you to email me an update each hour of the school day from 8 am to 3 pm, let my kid do whatever they want in your class, including sleeping or using their phone, they don't have to do homework or take tests, but you'll still give them an "A" for all the trouble you've caused.
>
> **Teacher:** How am I supposed to do that?
>
> **Parent:** I don't care. You're the teacher. Just do it.
>
> **Teacher:** Do you realize if I did that, it would not only go against my personal and professional standards, morals, and ethics but would ultimately be cheating your kid and could mean they have to repeat the class? So again, let's work together and find a solution that's realistic and

works for everyone, especially your kid. "How can we realistically fix this?"

Parent: Well...I guess I would just like to know how my kid is doing more often, instead of finding out when it's too late. I realize you're busy and can't contact me all the time and that I need to do a better job of checking my texts and emails.

Table 11.7: Step 4

Step 4: Find the Fix "What does fixed look like?"
"What does fixed look like to you?"
"In a perfect world, what does fixed look like to you?"
"How am I supposed to do that?"
"Do you realize if...?"
"How can we realistically fix this?"

Similar to how the lesson plans we put on paper rarely go as planned in the real world, the same is true when applying this template. As a result, you might have to revisit a previous step before moving on. For example, after asking *"How can we realistically fix this?"* the parent replies, *"You can fix this by doing what I want"*, then it might be helpful to return to previous steps or use a combination thereof and respond with *"I know it probably seems like I'm out to get you or your kid but I'm not. I want to help them succeed. It sounds like you also want them to succeed, so how can we work to fix this?"*

Step 5: Listen and Lean In

After initially hearing what "fixed looks like," it's important to continue to listen and lean into their suggestions and concerns (while asking for clarification) to ensure you are now both working to be part of the solution and, for the most part, have moved beyond the problem.

While I'm not an expert on body language, experience suggests that you will know when you have moved into this step (the home stretch of the process) because the other person will do something to indicate they are less guarded and more relaxed. For example, they might sit back and relax more in their chair or uncross their arms. Depending upon how you are located in the room, they might literally lean closer by putting their arms on the table, suggesting a "let's roll up our sleeves and get to work" mentality. If you are meeting over the phone, you will hear a change in their tone, it will become more conversational and less defensive.

The key phrase in Step 5 is asking them "*What would you like to see?*" Notice the use of the personal pronoun since this should not make them defensive and clearly gives them the invitation to offer what they want to see. In addition, it can be helpful to briefly summarize what you have agreed on to that point, using a "sounds like" phrase. For example, "Since it sounds like we both want your kid to be successful in my class, what would you like to see…"

> **Teacher:** *Since it sounds like we both want your kid to be successful in my class and agree communication is important, what would you like to see moving forward?*
>
> **Parent:** *I know you usually send emails, but text messages would be better. Doesn't the school have an application for that? Even if you could send me something once a week that would be great. Also, is there any way my kid could get some extra help?*

Table 11.8: Step 5

Step 5: Listen and Lean In *"What would you like to see?"*
"What would you like to see happen moving forward to ensure your kid is successful in my class?"

Please note that while it's possible they could re-visit a previous step and reply with an unrealistic response, by virtue of getting beyond Step 4 and into Step 5, it's highly unlikely. However, if they do throw you a curve ball, meet them in the step they are in and respond accordingly.

Step 6: Collaborate and Commit

As a teacher, you know the importance of a final check for understanding or an exit ticket to ensure that everyone got the message, is on the same page, and there will be no confusion. Step 6 essentially aims to accomplish this by providing some closure to the conversation along with a mutually agreed upon plan moving forward.

Based upon what was shared in the previous step, and building upon the other shared values, principles, or ideas that emerged in the conversation, come up with at least one actionable item that both parties can agree upon using "So, it sounds like we both..." This is even more effective if you proceed with a brief summary of what you already agree upon (see Table 11.9).

> ***Teacher:*** *Yes! We do have a text notification system in our gradebook app and any student can come to my room for extra help during our Study Periods on Tuesday and Thursday.*

So, it sounds like we both agree on a few things here. First of all, I'll send you weekly text updates about your kid's progress, and they're welcome to come to my Study Period. Also, I encourage all of my students to fill out their virtual planner with assignments and other important information, so please know that if you ask them to see it, it shouldn't be empty. Does this sound like a reasonable plan we can agree on?

Parent: *Yes. That sounds much better. I didn't know about the virtual planner so thanks for telling me. I appreciate your help.*

Table 11.9: Step 6

Step 6: Collaborate and Commit *"So, it sounds like be both..."*
"Since we both care about your kid's education and want them to be successful, it sounds like we both agree to touch base once a week and make sure your kid keeps their virtual planner up to date."

After you have verbalized what you both agree on, you could also suggest sending a follow-up email or text just to outline and document what was discussed. In addition, make sure to end the conversation on a positive note, continuing to reflect on who you are as a leader and recognizing you are always in the process of establishing relational equity with those you serve.

Tap Out Phrases

As previously mentioned, using this template is helpful but much like a classroom lesson, it's not possible to account for everything. Nonetheless, going into a conflict-based scenario with a plan – especially one you can practice or role-play ahead of time –is beneficial. However, despite your best efforts and intentions, the other person with whom you engage might become unreasonably angry, belligerent, or uncooperative.

Because of this, I suggest having a few "tap out phrases" you can say that will not only establish a boundary of what you are willing to accept (which also reflects your character) but also sends a clear message to the other person, while still being professional and allowing them the chance to continue with the conversation. Overall, please know you can always stop a conversation at any point, indicating it will be continued after you seek administrative input.

Table 11.10: Tap Out Phrases

Tap Out Phrases
"You're welcome to be a part of this conversation if…"
"I'm happy to continue this conversation if…"
"I will not tolerate…"

For example, if the other person makes a threat or uses hurtful language, you could reply as follows:

- "You're welcome to be a part of this conversation as long as you are able to use appropriate language."
- "I'm happy to continue this conversation as long as you choose to use respectful language."
- "My apologies for interrupting you, but I will not tolerate personal threats."
- "I'm happy to continue this conversation as long as you respect the fact that I will not tolerate those types of accusations against my character."

Addressing conflict, while never entirely comfortable, does become more manageable with practice. Although it's not natural for most humans to go around looking for difficult conversations, it's a necessary skill for all leaders, especially teachers. In addition, understanding that conflict is conflict can hopefully enable you to recognize you are capable of pursuing additional leadership roles outside of your classroom that will naturally require some level of having difficult conversations with colleagues, community members, or other stakeholders.

Discussion and Application Questions

1. Think about a conflict you have experienced. What aspects of the Pre-Conflict Checklist and "Likes" Template were and were not present? To what extent would the conflict have been more positive had it included more of the checklist and template?

2. Think about a potential conflict you might encounter with another adult as part of your role as a teacher (or use an actual scenario that is upcoming). Use the "Likes" Template to plan for this conversation. If possible, ask a trusted friend or colleague to role-play it with you.

3. Using the "Likes" Template, compose a conflict-based dialog between a teacher and a parent.

References

Brown, B. (2018). *Dare to lead: Brave work. Tough conversations. Whole hearts.* [Kindle *version*]. Random House. https://a.co/d/5C2eoSj

Dictionary.com. (n.d.). *Conflict.* In Dictionary.com https://www.dictionary.com/browse/conflict

Voss, C., & Raz, T. (2016). *Never split the difference: Negotiating as if your life depended on it.* [Kindle *version*]. Harper Business. https://a.co/d/bJTMY42

CHAPTER 12

Relational Realities of Leadership

―――◄ ►―――

"To handle yourself, use your head; to handle others, use your heart."
~Eleanor Roosevelt

As we've learned, leadership is multi-faceted, but at some level, it comes down to a relationship with another individual. Because of this, I have developed eight Relational Realities of Leadership based on my own experience and research. The purpose of these realities is to give you guidance and permission. Guidance as you continue in your leadership journey and permission to understand that sometimes, despite your best efforts, you might not always get it right or please everyone – including yourself. Nonetheless, you can still be an effective leader who builds trust, establishes healthy boundaries, adheres to core values, and fosters a positive organizational culture and climate through professional relationships. The Relational Realities of Leadership are as follows:

1. Control Yourself, Influence Others
2. Disappointment is not Detrimental
3. People Reflect and Project
4. Assurance through Abundance
5. Take Care, Not Caretaker
6. Narratives Nurture Notions
7. Two Truths, One Reality
8. Autonomy Allowed

Control Yourself, Influence Others
My personal definition and subsequent framework of leadership is influence through courage, character, relationships, and service. It's intentionally based upon the word influence because that's what leaders do: they influence others – individually and collectively – to modify their behavior, words, and ways of thinking. In addition, leaders essentially influence others with their "hands in their pockets," meaning they

figuratively and literally cannot physically force another person to do something they don't want to do.

As a teacher, have you ever taken the time to reflect on the fact that you accomplish great things with your students – you significantly inspire their actions and development – entirely through relational and social influence? This is true for all leaders across all organizations, yet again, something educators inherently understand.

Whatever moves the needle, whatever gets people to progress from one point to the next (increased learning, improved sales, positive morale, etc.) happens in the absence of true force and relies on relational influence. Granted, teachers and leaders can impose undesirable consequences, but ultimately, we can't ethically (or legally) force another human being to do something they don't want to do.

Although some of you may have already come to this realization, it's nonetheless important to note because as a leader, the only person over whom you have any control is yourself – everything else is influence. And although this makes sense in terms of positively influencing others, it also serves as a reminder that while it's frustrating when people don't respond accordingly to our influence, it's futile to waste time worrying about it.

While we can control our actions and strive to lead with integrity, aligning with our character and core values, there will always be individuals who choose not to engage, share the vision, or cooperate. Their resistance is not necessarily a reflection of our leadership ability but often stems from their own personal choices, external circumstances, or differing perspectives.

Disappointment is not Detrimental

I imagine a significant reason you chose to become a teacher is that at your core, you genuinely care about people and feel a deep, perhaps even inherent, desire or calling to help others. You are driven to serve and, at times, to solve problems for those around you, which is why I consider teaching one of the quintessential helping professions.

Based on my experience as a teacher and my work training future educators and current leaders, I would also guess you possess a strong sense of empathy and an ability to read the room, quickly sensing how others are feeling, which can be helpful when inside your classroom. However, because of this, you are likely to feel a deep need to fix things for others, stepping in to help when something feels off or unresolved. You probably also don't like upsetting, hurting, or disappointing others – not only because you can sense their emotions but because, as a genuinely kind person, you strive to ensure others don't experience negative feelings because of your actions.

Think of a time when you had to hold a student accountable by enforcing a classroom or school policy but still felt bad or at least a little anxious at the thought of upsetting the student or their parents. In addition, have you ever been in a professional situation in which you knew that doing the right thing would also upset a colleague, perhaps someone you consider a friend?

While it's understandable – and commendable – that we don't enjoy or look forward to upsetting other people, here's a powerful truth: disappointing another person and causing them to feel less than positive emotions is neither your fault nor is it detrimental to the other person. Temporary disappointment seldom equates to long-term harm. Human beings, especially adults, are fully capable of being disappointed.

In fact, whether it's a classroom teacher with their students or a principal with their staffulty, there is not a single district, state, or federal law or any part of a negotiated agreement or union handbook that says, "*Thou shall not disappoint or upset another human.*" Yes, I understand that in the event people actually violate a law or policy, it may very well disappoint another person, but in these cases, there's obviously more to the story and certainly feelings and emotions beyond disappointment.

Therefore, if doing your job (teaching, enforcing policies, grading fairly, benching an athlete for making a poor choice, being honest, having integrity, holding other adults accountable…) means another person gets upset, that's not your fault. Most of the time, the other person made one or more choices and behaved their way into the negative consequences and subsequent disappointment. In fact, their disappointment is usually because they either got caught and are being held accountable or because they simply didn't get their way.

Nonetheless, I realize that many of us who went into teaching are natural people pleasers, and this is hard to hear and even more difficult to implement, but it's as true as it is effective and therapeutic. It's not your job – in any professional position within any industry – to make sure people are always happy and never experience any negative feelings. In fact, allowing students (or an administrator allowing their staffulty) to experience a reasonable amount of disappointment can be a valuable lesson. It teaches that we can't always shield those we serve from the consequences of their choices or the realities of the world around them.

People Reflect and Project

After reading the previous section, you might be thinking "*I understand I can't always please everyone, and it's not my fault if they're disappointed, especially if they behaved their way into the situation, but that still doesn't keep them from being mean to me, spreading gossip, not wanting to sit at my lunch table, and so on. What am I supposed to do about this?*"

That's a great question and one I wish I would have learned the response to earlier in my teaching career. In fact, I don't think I fully came to appreciate this notion until after I became a titled leader. Remember, you can only control yourself and influence others. In addition, you cannot be held responsible every time someone you serve gets upset, angry, or disappointed. Furthermore, you are also not responsible for the words, actions, and tactics they use as a result of you doing your job and them being upset ("*You made me mad, which then caused me to say those words – it's all your fault!*")

In his book *Winning with People: Discover the People Principles that Work for You Every Time*, John Maxwell (2007) introduces the Pain Principle, which states, "Hurting people hurt people and are easily hurt by them" (p. 23). While you may have encountered this idea before, it serves as a powerful reminder that you cannot always control – or be responsible for – how others choose to interpret and react to certain situations. (As we will learn in another Relational Reality, you can also neither control nor be responsible for the subsequent stories and narratives people choose to believe or tell themselves.)

Please note this relational reality refers to "hurting people," which isn't synonymous with bad people or flawed people. Remember that leaders are in the people business, people are messy, and leaders are also people. Nonetheless, this serves as a reminder that when up against adversity or negative consequences, what often emerges from most people – what they reflect and project onto others – is usually reflective of the feelings and emotions they have inside.

Assurance Through Abundance

Have you ever worked in an organization in which it felt as though no good deed went unpunished or as if there was a scarcity mentality in that only a few people could be successful? Or perhaps you've experienced this mindset with certain individuals who, despite the positive organizational culture and climate, might personally feel offended if they either can't win or someone else is recognized.

In the 30th Anniversary Edition of his bestselling book *The 7 Habits of Highly Effective People* (2020), Stephen Covey introduces the concept of the Abundance Mentality, describing it as "the paradigm that there is plenty out there and enough to spare for everybody. It results in sharing of prestige, of recognition, of profits, of decision making. It opens possibilities, options, alternatives, and creativity" (pp. 250–251).

Leaders must understand – and promote the vision – that recognition, success, and opportunities are not finite resources; there is more than enough to go around. Simply put, it's not just acceptable but essential to cheer for, support, and celebrate others' successes!

It's also important to recognize that when an individual or an organizational culture (which is usually a reflection of its leader) possesses and promotes a scarcity mentality, it can often be indicative of how they feel about themselves, usually rooted in a sense of inadequacy or always needing to prove oneself. Because of this, it's important for leaders to both send and live the message that "I'm enough. You're enough. We're enough."

Providing this assurance through abundance can help those you serve feel valued, seen, and heard while also promoting an environment of mutual respect, confidence, and support.

Take Care, Not Caretaker

As previously mentioned, due to their kind hearts and inherent desire to serve others, teachers and those in other helping professions – with the best of intentions – may believe that "helping" equates to "fixing." Additionally, while helping others does require a certain amount of care established through some form of a relationship, we must set personal boundaries.

I have no doubt you have already learned this and perhaps continue to struggle with the notion of when and where to set those boundaries with your students because as your kids, you genuinely care about them, want what's best for them, and your heart hurts when unfortunate things happen outside of school, and you can't help them or fix it.

I can share from personal experience that if you are a teacher at heart, if you leave the classroom to pursue more formalized leadership roles, as long as you take your character, integrity, and heart with you, you will feel the same about your "new students," who are the adults you now serve. While we recognize the challenges faced by PreK-12 students are uniquely nuanced by the fact that they are minors, it's important to remember adults also bring their own personal issues, struggles, and experiences that can deeply affect you. Moreover, adults who are unhappy or facing difficulties in their personal lives may, without realizing it, seek to fill a void or address unmet needs through their work lives.

However, part of taking care of yourself as a leader is realizing you must establish clear boundaries – with yourself and others.

While leaders should genuinely care about and *professionally take care* of those they serve, they are not their *personal caretakers*. This fundamental distinction reminds us to strike a crucial balance of supporting others' professional growth and well-being while recognizing we are not responsible for their personal lives and the extent to which they, as individuals outside of work, find joy, satisfaction, and fulfillment.

This boundary safeguards both the leader and those they lead, promoting independence over dependence and growth over enabling. While, as leaders, our professional actions can influence someone's personal life, we are not responsible for solving personal problems, managing emotions, or ensuring others' personal and private happiness.

Narratives Nurture Notions

As we explored in the previous chapter on addressing conflict, people often create narratives –stories they tell themselves – that, while not entirely accurate, can significantly influence their behavior and how they reflect and project onto others. The saying "perception is everything" is fitting here because individuals tend to believe and act upon the narrative that is either most prevalent or conveniently aligns with their existing beliefs or way of thinking.

This is a crucial relational reality for leaders. While fostering an environment that promotes accurate narratives is valuable, people may still choose to embrace and act on false narratives despite a leader's best efforts. These narratives shape their notions – beliefs, and perceptions – and can drive actions that are often difficult to predict or influence.

Furthermore, as we have learned in previous Relational Realities, as a leader, you are not responsible for the extent to which someone chooses to believe and act upon inaccurate narratives. As I mentioned at the beginning of this chapter, the two primary purposes of these realities are to provide you with both guidance and permission.

In the case of this reality, the guidance is to focus on creating an organizational culture and climate that promotes truth and clarity while understanding you cannot control others' perceptions. The permission is to release yourself from the burden of worrying about and trying to manage or correct every false narrative –your role is to courageously influence, not to shoulder responsibility for the stories others choose to tell themselves and their subsequent behaviors.

Two Truths, One Reality
As educators who are in the people business, we understand that not only is nobody perfect but human beings can be very unpredictable. While certainly outside of the scope of this book, if you are familiar with statistical analysis within the Social Sciences, to which education belongs, there's a reason why a relatively small number can be statistically significant when looking at certain measures such as correlation: there are always multiple variables and moving parts involved with people.

Because of this, it's important for leaders to understand and appreciate that within their organizations, there can be multiple truths within the same reality. In other words, leaders need to acknowledge that two things can be true at the same time. Embracing this Relational Reality will again provide guidance and understanding along with permission.

For instance, have you ever known a colleague who excelled as a classroom teacher but transitioned into administration – possibly prematurely or for the wrong reasons – and, if you're being honest, didn't perform as well in that role? If so, you may have found it difficult to acknowledge their shortcomings in one area because of their strengths in another. You might have even felt that admitting they weren't a great administrator somehow diminished their teaching abilities or even suggested they weren't a good person, which clearly wasn't true. It's as if we adopt this rigid, binary mindset, which is often verbalized as "I feel bad admitting this because they're such a nice person and they mean well, but *Mr. Soandso* is really struggling in their new job."

Have you ever known a teacher who was exceptional in their classroom with students but, for some reason, was unpleasant or even toxic among their colleagues? (This is atypical in the real world, but I'm using it for instructional purposes.) While it's relatively easy to acknowledge the two truths, one reality in the first scenario where a good person simply took on the wrong role, this situation feels more challenging yet is equally relevant for leaders.

When someone we don't personally care for is publicly recognized, our instinct may be to question it: *"How could that be? How can someone who treats their colleagues this way win an award?"* This reaction stems from an all-or-nothing mindset that oversimplifies complex realities.

As leaders, we must accept that multiple truths can coexist, even when they're uncomfortable or inconvenient. In this scenario, the two truths we must accept are that *Mr. Award Winner* can be both an outstanding teacher and an unpleasant presence in faculty meetings. Recognizing these dual truths doesn't diminish our standards; it reflects our maturity and capacity for nuance as leaders. Furthermore, it serves as a powerful reminder that leaders are called to serve and influence everyone with character and courage grounded in professional relationships.

Please note this relational reality does not grant leaders permission to adopt a laissez-faire approach; it doesn't mean they are soft, nor does it absolve others of accountability for failing to meet expectations or exhibiting poor behavior. However, it does mean leaders must balance holding others accountable with empathy and fairness, understanding their influence is built upon relationships, not control, and true leadership requires navigating this delicate balance with wisdom and integrity.

Autonomy Allowed

In the Disappointment is Not Detrimental reality, we explored the importance of understanding and granting yourself permission as a leader to disappoint or upset others; disappointment is a natural part of life, and adults are capable of handling it. While the guidance and permission offered by this reality may provide confidence, clarity, and courage, it's essential to recognize that it works both ways.

As someone in the people business, you will inevitably find yourself on the receiving end of someone else's undesirable behavior. You'll feel angry, upset, or frustrated, and your instinctive reactions might include thoughts like, *"How dare they do that!"* or *"Don't they realize how that makes me feel?"* or even, *"I bet they did that just to make me mad!"* While these thoughts may feel valid, they often reflect the story you're choosing to tell yourself about the other person.

Even if your assumptions turn out to be true, here's a reality check: *They're allowed!* People have autonomy. They're allowed to make decisions, behave in ways you dislike, or even upset you – whether it is intentional or not. While they are not free from the consequences of their actions, their autonomy remains intact, and as a leader, your role is to once again understand and navigate these dynamics with courage, character, and professionalism.

In more practical terms, it can actually be somewhat therapeutic – perhaps saying the *second thing that comes to mind* – by simply telling ourselves, "They're allowed!" For example, it's 3:58 pm, and the faculty meeting ends at 4:00 pm, and someone asks a question everyone knows will take more than two minutes to address. While there are many tactics the meeting leader could use to address this, the reality is, they're allowed to ask the question. It doesn't mean they're making us all happy by doing it, but they're still allowed.

Think about other situations or behaviors in which reminding yourself "they're allowed" could have been beneficial. How might this mindset have influenced your thoughts, actions, and words, as well as the responses of the other person? To what extent could the outcome have been different? Reflect on these scenarios and identify recurring behaviors where recognizing, respecting, and allowing others' autonomy could help you better understand others while setting a healthy boundary for yourself.

I hope these eight Relational Realities of Leadership were able to meet you where you're at, regardless of your professional experience or career trajectory, and add value to you as well as those you serve, be it students, colleagues, parents, or other stakeholders. As we've learned, relationships are foundational to influencing and leading others, which must start with the relationship we have with ourselves.

Whether you're leading from the classroom or a formal administrative role, these realities give you both guidance and permission: guidance to navigate complex interpersonal dynamics with character, courage, and compassion, and permission to accept that you're only human and neither can nor should be able to please everyone all the time.

Remember, at its core, leadership is fundamentally about influence – the ability to positively impact others through our words, actions, and examples. As teachers, you already understand this truth because you live it daily in your classrooms, influencing students' lives through courage, character, relationships, and service. In this way, every teacher is inherently a leader, making our profession not just a career choice but a powerful opportunity to shape the future through meaningful relationships and purposeful influence.

Discussion and Application Questions

1. For each of the eight Relational Realities, write a brief reflection in which you assess your personal comfort level, experience, or need for growth as a leader.
2. To what extent have you worked with leaders who are either proficient with the Relational Realities or perhaps deficient in a few areas? How did this affect or contribute to your job satisfaction and engagement and the culture and climate of the organization?

References

Covey, S. R. (2020). *The 7 habits of highly effective people: 30th anniversary edition.* [Kindle version]. Simon & Schuster. https://a.co/d/fBfji0W

Maxwell, J. C. (2007). Winning with people: Discover the people principles that work for you every time. [Kindle version]. HarperCollins Leadership. https://a.co/d/3KqphM5

CONCLUSION

Anytime I am given the awesome opportunity and responsibility of adding value to others and those they serve through leadership training and development, my overarching goal is to provide them with permission and perspective.

I hope that as a professional educator, I have given you permission to continue on your journey as an influential leader. Regardless of whether you move into formalized roles or remain in the awesome position of a classroom teacher, please know you are uniquely called and qualified to lead and inspire students, colleagues, and community members *on a daily basis*.

Additionally, I hope that through our time together within the pages of this book I have offered you a new or enhanced perspective, based on the foundational principle that *all teachers are leaders*! Among the many superpowers you possess and express each day, please know that regardless of your title, *you are an exceptional leader*; you influence others by serving them with courage and character, built upon a sound foundation of authentic relationships.

As I write this, I also feel uniquely fortunate to have the benefit of hindsight and experience. Since writing the previous chapters, I have continued to share and teach these concepts to hundreds of educators across the country and even as part of a destination leadership workshop in Costa Rica. I have also spent time training and developing leaders outside of education in the corporate space, further reinforcing the value and applicability of what we have learned.

Personal Reflection and Application

As educators, we continue to refine our lesson plans and classroom practice based upon the real-time feedback we receive from the field with the ultimate goal of maximizing our impact on student achievement.

Discovering Leadership Identity

I wrote this book because I firmly believe *all teachers are leaders*, and by helping them uncover and utilize these inherent talents (providing permission and perspective), we can accomplish great things such as positively affecting student achievement, increasing teachers' job satisfaction, boosting organizational morale, and improving teacher retention, to name a few.

Reflection and Application Questions

1. How has this process enabled you to discover your own leadership identity?
2. Provide an example of one behavior (i.e., daily habit) you can implement or share with others that aligns with discovering one's leadership identity as a professional educator.

Professional Growth and Purpose

I've often said that if there are two groups of educators who are on the edge of making a significant career decision that will take them out of the classroom, I'm hopeful that understanding the value of developing themselves as leaders will enable them to make an informed decision. Imagine a bell curve that represents the general population of classroom teachers in which those on the far-left side are contemplating leaving the classroom and profession altogether, and those on the far-right side are trying to decide if they should leave the classroom to pursue formal or titled leadership opportunities.

As previously mentioned, having been able to apply the principles in this book, I am confident that developing and empowering teacher leaders can help keep some teachers in the classroom by giving them a renewed sense of professional purpose and perspective, thus contributing to student achievement by supporting teacher retention and overall job satisfaction.

Additionally, we also need excellent educators in formalized administrative roles to serve students through providing organizational leadership to their respective schools, districts, and communities. While leaving the classroom can be a difficult decision for any teacher, providing teacher leadership training can serve as the necessary catalyst to help teachers decide if they can best serve students through classroom instruction or building or district-level leadership.

Finally, referring to the bell curve analogy, training teacher leaders also empowers the majority of educators – who are most likely not on the verge of leaving the classroom to pursue administration or another career – to also have a renewed sense of purpose by enabling them to pursue informal leadership opportunities outside of their respective classrooms.

Reflection and Application Questions
1. Where are you on the bell curve of classroom teachers?
2. What types of professional (or personal) permission and perspective has studying teacher leadership given you in terms of your overall career trajectory and job satisfaction?
3. Provide an example of one behavior or daily habit you can implement or share with others that aligns with your overall professional growth and purpose.

Practical Applications

As a former classroom teacher and now as someone who works with both future and current teachers and administrators across the country, I know your time is valuable. In addition, I realize that while you recognize the importance of professional development – whether it occurs as an in-service during the school year or is part of a class, workshop, or book study – it needs to be practical, relevant, and professional.

Let's be honest, most of the time when you are asked to engage in professional development, it's on a school day without kids in the building which means you would much rather be in your classroom working! Add to that the ever-present fear that you will show up and be asked to do yet another get-to-know-your-partner ice breaker, followed by being engaged in activities you might dislike while learning something that may not directly apply to your classroom and students. Because of these experiences, it's understandable why some teachers view professional development as adding one more thing to their busy schedules.

However, just as those of you with coaching experience wouldn't consider weightlifting and proper nutrition as burdens piled onto your athletes' plates, effective professional development shouldn't be viewed as an add-on or yet another thing for educators to endure. For your athletes, consistent training and healthy habits are essential to build strength, prevent injury, and enhance performance.

Similarly, when teachers engage in meaningful professional development – the kind that's thoughtfully designed, appropriately delivered, and aligned with student success – it serves as a form of professional conditioning that builds teachers' capacity rather than depleting it. In other words, it *adds to their strengths*, not their busy schedules and full plates.

Reflection and Application Questions

1. List 3-5 practical ideas or initiatives you can use or initiate in your classroom, school, or district.
2. Reflecting on what you listed in the previous question, to what extent will these ideas or initiatives impact or be associated with student achievement?
3. Provide an example of one behavior or habit you can implement or share with others that aligns with one of your identified practical applications.

Personal Impact

As I said previously, leadership is leadership. This not only reinforces the notion that anyone who routinely influences others in a people business is a leader, but due to their daily, minute-by-minute human influence, teachers are the epitome of servant leaders. Accordingly, while we may use the term *professional development*, the reality is that in a people-centered, performance-based profession such as education, we are more appropriately engaged in the process of *personal development*; we must develop and lead ourselves before we can serve others.

Therefore, while I'm confident you can apply the various leadership principles in this book to your classroom, I'm also hopeful they will help you in other areas outside of the classroom, such as within your school, district, and community.

Reflection and Application Questions

1. Thinking about your personal development as a leader, and its subsequent impact on your professional practice, which areas were strengthened or reinforced? In which areas did you grow and learn the most?

2. Provide an example of one behavior you can implement or share with others that aligns with one of your identified areas of personal impact.

Final Thoughts

As our time together comes to an end, I would like to leave you with a few final thoughts that will hopefully encourage you to continue your own leadership journey growth while also coming alongside someone else and sharing what you have learned.

Keep Learning, Growing, and Influencing

As an educator, you understand the importance of continued growth and lifelong learning based on a growth mindset. Therefore, I hope what we have learned together will serve as the beginning of your ongoing leadership journey; I encourage you to consider the following steps.

Start Small: Choose one concept from this book that particularly resonated with you and represents an identified area of growth and commit to implementing it for a specific timeframe, such as one month, a semester, or the entire school year. Remember, leadership is developed daily, not in a day; consistency is more important than perfection.

Document Your Impact: Keep a leadership journal noting how these concepts affect your daily interactions with students, colleagues, and stakeholders along with any new ideas or realizations. You might be surprised by how much you are already influencing others outside of your classroom.

Seek Opportunities: Look for ways to contribute to the overall culture and climate of your school, district or community through formal or informal leadership. Even small acts of service and influence can create significant ripple effects throughout your school, district, and community.

The Multiplier Effect of Teacher Leadership

I believe our network of colleagues contributes to our professional and relational net worth, which underscores the value of continued growth, development, and mentoring. Furthermore, I define legacy as the extent to which we influence people we will never meet. Accordingly, do what my friend Brad Black (2024) says in his book, *Talent, Culture, and Teams: The Ex-Factors of Excellence*, by "selecting one more like the best" (p. 85). Multiply yourself, your *network,* and your *net worth* by developing, encouraging, and mentoring another teacher leader. Give them the necessary permission and perspective to lean into their inherent leadership abilities, thus impacting students, colleagues, stakeholders, and others whom you will never meet.

End of Class; Start of the Journey

Throughout my career teaching future and current educators, when our classes conclude at the end of the semester, I always tell my students that, in many ways, our journey has just begun and I hope we can stay in touch. I give them my contact information and let them know we are now colleagues and to contact me if they ever need anything or if I can be of assistance.

Likewise, even though our time together in this book has come to an end I hope our shared journey has just begun. As your colleague, as someone who believes in your abilities to positively influence those you serve, we are now part of each other's network, and I would be honored to continue to learn from one another as you will most certainly add to my net worth. Therefore, I hope you update me on your leadership journey, and let me know if you ever need anything (chris@cjleadership.com). Additionally, because I value your input, perspective and expertise, please let me know the extent to which the concepts in this book were helpful, in need of revision, or should be reconsidered for future publications.

I would also like to say Thank You for serving your students, schools and communities each and every day. You matter, and you are making a difference, the type that oftentimes comes with a delayed return on investment in the form of an adult telling you you're the reason they stayed in school, felt valued, seen, and heard, continued to study a certain subject or even decided to become a teacher.

We've explored why teaching is fundamentally about leadership and influence. As educator Glennice Harmon (1948) eloquently expressed many years ago, "They ask me why I teach and I reply, 'Where could I find more splendid company?'" (p. 375). If you ask me why I'm passionate about working with educators such as yourself to help you uncover your inherent leadership abilities that not only helps you – personally and professionally – but also supports your students, colleagues, and communities, I also reply with "Where could I find more splendid company?" Remember, as a professional educator, regardless of where your career takes you, you're already a phenomenal leader where you are; you don't have to leave to lead.

References

Black, B. (2024). *Talent, culture, and teams: The eX Factors of Excellence.* Streamline.

Harmon, G. L. (1948, September). They ask me why I teach. *NEA Journal, 37*(1), 375.

ACKNOWLEDGEMENTS

I would like to thank my students for making this book possible. Teaching the leadership class to both future and current educators over the past five years has been educational and rewarding. Through personal correspondence and course evaluations, students shared that the lessons were transformational to their classroom practice and overall professional development, often suggesting I write a book to capture the philosophical principles, frameworks, discussions, and activities from our class.

I'm also grateful to the building and district-level administrators who have trusted me to provide leadership training to their faculty, staff, and leadership teams. Working with educators within different schools and districts has been both humbling and enlightening. Their experiences and feedback illustrate how these leadership principles have positively impacted their professional practice and school communities.

ABOUT THE AUTHOR

Dr. Christopher J. Jochum is the founder and CEO of CJ Leadership Solutions, LLC. As a sought-after speaker, trainer, and coach who believes that leadership is about influence rather than formal titles, Chris partners with organizations in the United States and abroad to transform their culture and climate by developing leadership capacity within the entire organization. He is also a Professor and Chair of the Department of Teacher Education at Fort Hays State University, where he leads a large teacher preparation program. His career, spanning close to three decades in K-12 and higher education, began in the public schools teaching Spanish and English as a Second Language before holding faculty appointments at the University of Central Missouri and the University of Nebraska at Kearney. His research focuses on leadership development in both K-12 and higher education, as well as the value of study abroad. Chris hosts "The Department Chair Leadership Podcast" and is the author of "The Department Chair: A Practical Guide to Effective Leadership."

Bring Chris to Your School or Event

Whether you're planning a professional development day, leadership conference, organizational retreat, or strategic planning session — Chris brings clarity, purpose, and transformative insight to every engagement.

As a speaker, trainer, coach, author, and educator, Chris works with K-12 schools, higher education institutions, and corporate teams to equip leaders with the clarity, skills, and frameworks they need to define compelling mission statements, develop applicable and sustainable core values, and create thriving organizational culture and climate. Chris also trains leaders to build leadership capacity within their own teams, creating a multiplier effect that strengthens organizations from the inside out.

Chris is available for:

- Keynote speaking
- Professional development
- Executive and team coaching
- Leadership development training and retreats
- Mission statement development
- Culture, climate, and core values development
- Organizational culture and climate consulting
- Conflict management workshops and coaching

From classrooms to boardrooms, Chris invests in organizations and those they serve through real-world, applicable strategies that create lasting impact.

To inquire about availability or to start a conversation, visit cjleadership.com or email Chris at chris@cjleadership.com

MORE BOOKS BY ROAD TO AWESOME

Taking the Leap: A Field Guide for Aspiring School Leaders by Robert F. Breyer

Transform: Techy Notes to Make Learning Sticky by Debbie Tannenbaum

Becoming Principal: A Leadership Journey & The Story of School Community by Dr. Jeff Prickett

Elevate Your Vibe: Action Planning with Purpose by Lisa Toebben

#OwnYourEpic: Leadership Lessons in Owning Your Voice and Your Story by Dr. Jay Dostal

The Design Thinking, Entrepreneurial, Visionary Planning Leader: A Practical guide for Thriving in Ambiguity by Dr. Michael Nagler

Becoming the Change: Five Essential Elements to Being Your Best Self by Dan Wolfe

inspired: moments that matter by Melissa Wright

Foundations of Instructional Coaching: Impact People, Improve Instruction, Increase Success by Ashley Hubner

Out of the Trenches: Stories of Resilient Educators
by Dana Goodier

Principled Leader
by Bobby Pollicino

Road to Awesome: The Journey of a Leader
by Darrin Peppard

When Calling Parents Isn't Your Calling:
A teacher's guide to communicating with all parents
by Crystal Frommert

Struggle to Strength:
Finding the Ingredients to Your Secret Sauce
by Kip Shubert

Guiding Transformational Change in Education
by Kristina V. Mattis

Be the Cause: An Educator's Guide to EFFECTive Instruction
by Josh Korb

Called to Empower
by Coach Kurt Hines

The Blueprint: Survive and Thrive as a School Administrator
by Todd M. Bloomer

Sustaining Excellence: How Culture Drives Teacher Retention
by Martin Silverman

Lead with HOPE: Building a System of Self-Efficacy
by Dr. Brandi Kelly

Frogs and Crayons
by Geoffrey May

~~stressed~~ Leaders: Stay in the Game
by Dan Stecken

Racing the Future
by Brad Waid

CHILDREN'S BOOKS FROM ROAD TO AWESOME

Road to Awesome A Journey for Kids
by Jillian DuBois and Darrin M. Peppard

Emersyn Blake and the Spotted Salamander
by Kim Collazo

Theodore Edward Makes a New Friend
by Alyssa Schmidt

I'm Autistic and I'm Awesome
by Derek Danziger

Emersyn Blake and the Stalked Jellyfish
by Kim Collazo

Birdie & Mipps
by Barbara Gruener

Teddy the Tiny Tree
by Derek Danziiger

Knit Back Together
by Barbara Gruener

roadtoawesome.net/books

www.ingramcontent.com/pod-product-compliance
Lightning Source LLC
Chambersburg PA
CBHW050105170426
43198CB00014B/2464